MEMORIES
OF LONG POND

MEMORIES
OF LONG POND
NORTHWOOD, NEW HAMPSHIRE

IRENE E. DUPONT

iUniverse, Inc.
Bloomington

MEMORIES OF LONG POND
Northwood, New Hampshire

iUniverse books may be ordered through booksellers or by contacting:

iUniverse
1663 Liberty Drive
Bloomington, IN 47403
www.iuniverse.com
1-800-Authors (1-800-288-4677)

ISBN: 978-1-4759-6290-1 (sc)
ISBN: 978-1-4759-6291-8 (ebk)

Library of Congress Control Number: 2012922165

Printed in the United States of America

iUniverse rev. date: 11/19/2012

CONTENTS

We do not remember days—We remember moments

Irene E. DuPont
Manchester, NH 03102

FOREWORD

The Northwood Historical Society is grateful to Irene E. DuPont for this history of the development of Long Pond Estates, a real service to the town of Northwood and to the residents of Long Pond Estates.

The development now known as Long Pond Estates was once a part of the James farm. This large tract of land was settled at the end of the Revolutionary War by James Stevens James. Many years later, in 1850, the farm was purchased by his grandson, Samuel Shepherd James, who farmed and forested there until his death in 1907.

Samuel Shepherd James wrote in his diary, really a work journal, every day from 1839 until just a few weeks before his death. Through the many entries we know what he did all year, year after year, in all the parts of his farm, including the fields and woodlots around Long Pond.

Samuel Shepherd James was a record keeper. He would be so pleased and we are, too, to know the record keeping continues.

Northwood Historical Society

ACKNOWLEDGMENTS

I want to thank my husband, Paul, for his love and unwavering support during all of the time I spent over the last four years in gathering the information needed to complete this book. Thanks go to my friend Nancy Rousselle for overseeing my written words. Thanks to Thelma Donnelly, my wonderful sister, for her support and offering of constructive advice. I want to thank my son-in-law, Gary Tasker, who supplied many old postcards from his collection regarding the Tasker family, who has resided in the Northwood area for many years. Thank you to the friends at Ritz Camera in Manchester, New Hampshire, for all their assistance with the printing of many photographs used in this book. I also want to thank Joann Weeks Bailey for all her help in recovering the past, along with others from the Northwood Historical Society. Finally, I want to extend special gratitude and sincere thanks to all the friends, neighbors, and property owners of Long Pond who have allowed me to write about their lives and property.

INTRODUCTION

Long Pond is a 101.9 acre spring-fed lake tucked away in the town of Northwood, New Hampshire. The James family owned the entire lake from the 1800s until 1960, when Maurice James decided to sell the land on his side to a developer. Lots were quickly established and sold to people wanting a summer cottage. Thirty-eight years ago, the DuPont family of five purchased a camp on Long Pond to enjoy swimming, hiking, fishing, and just getting away from the city. They continue to use their seasonal home today.

Memories of Long Pond tells the story of the James family, the DuPont family, and many other cottage owners, as well as the many changes that have occurred at this body of water over the years. This is a wonderful look at the history and growth of this area in Northwood, New Hampshire.

CHAPTER 1

STARTED WITH A HEADACHE

It all started with a headache. It was a Sunday, and we were with a real estate agent out looking for a cottage on a body of water in the woods. We had decided that when we sold my husband's home in Allenstown, we would begin to look for a getaway camp. At this point, we had been looking for two years, and now going into the third year, we could not find anything that was worth what we were willing to pay. But on this particular day, we had this appointment with the Realtor on Route 4, and we were hopeful. He had shown us two places already that we were not really interested in. One place had a small stream flowing through the cellar way, making the cottage very damp. That was on Pleasant Lake. The other one was on Northwood Lake, but throughout the winter, you had to place a beam in the middle of the ceiling to prevent the roof from caving in. There was one more that we had to see, and I still had a splitting headache and upset stomach. I wanted to go home, but the Realtor and my husband convinced me to see just one more lake cottage. This one had just been placed on the market, and even the Realtor hadn't seen it yet.

So I said, "Okay, but that's it—home we go after that." We proceeded down a dirt road and traveled about three-fourths of a mile. Then we stopped at a small opening on the left. Getting out of the vehicle, I saw it was all overgrown, and the house was all boarded up. The Realtor opened a wooden door that reminded me of a barricade to a fort, then he unlocked the next door. It was sparsely furnished and quite dark inside; all the windows were closed with a pressed board. He found the electric box and turned on the lights. It had two bedrooms, a full bath, a nice kitchen open to the family room, a screened porch, and a fireplace. Paul looked at me and said, "Wow!"

Paul went under the place and then remarked how well the cottage was built. We could not see the water due to the overgrowth of trees and bushes. We did, however, go down the path to see the body of water, and it looked great. There were not many camps on the other side, but there were a lot of rocks on the shore and it had a very rocky bottom. The water appeared exceptionally clean, not swampy at all.

We didn't say much to the Realtor at this point, except that we would get back to him. We left and talked all the way home about how great this place was. When we arrived home, we called the Realtor and said we would call the bank and see him again that upcoming Monday.

We decided that if the price was right, we would take it, but first we had to check with the banker, Earnest Coloumb, regarding a mortgage and other costs.

On Monday we went to the Suncook Bank and talked with Ernie. He said to offer $2,000 less and see what the owners would do. We did so, and the Realtor picked up the phone and called the owner in Florida. He spoke with Mr. Stickles regarding our offer. Stickles replied asking, "Do they have children?" We did, in fact, have five children, who would all thoroughly enjoy the camp and the water. He quickly replied, "It's a deal."

That started the *Memories of Long Pond*.

The abstract of the title was produced and given to us. It read:

> Property of Harold E. and Lucille M. Stickle situated in Northwood, New Hampshire, Estate of Orrin Moses James, born March 19, 1868, in Northwood, New Hampshire, the son to Samuel and Martha (Hill) James, died December 13, 1938. The will was approved January 3, 1940, by John A. Tasker, named executor. It read, devised, and bequeathed all property except property in Maine to his wife, Abbie A. L. James. The property of Long Pond was listed as 50 acres with no references. The inventory at that time fame listed real estate as $5,465.00, and personal estate, $2,139.23. The final account was filed and settled January 23, 1940. The property was left to Leonard F. Giles. Then, February 24, 1955, it was left to Ruby M. and Gerald H. Giles (brother). On March 8, 1949, it was then deeded to Leonard F. Giles and Ruby Giles; a right-of-way was deeded to Long Pond Estates, Inc., March 27, 1962. On November 28, 1961, Elizabeth Gratke, Jewel Strickland, and Robert Strickland received the deed and abstract of the property. Paul and Irene E. DuPont purchased and received the deed in June 1975. A copy of the abstract is inserted further in the writing.

CHAPTER 2

HISTORY OF A NEW TOWN CALLED NORTHWOOD

The town of Northwood was barely formed when the colonies began their fight for independence from the British; Northwood men and women assumed their full share of suffering and sacrifices of those trying years.

Following the Revolutionary War, Northwood shared in what is sometimes called the new country's era. The nation grew and prospered, and Northwood did, too. Prosperity was assured by the building of the Portsmouth and Concord Turnpike about 1800. Portsmouth was then the gateway to New Hampshire, and the turnpike became the main artery of communication with the interior. Its location on this route gave Northwood a decided advantage, opening an outlet for products, especially lumber.

As Northwood was about halfway between Concord and the coast, it was the place where travelers dined, where they had their teams rested and fed, and where they often slept. Responding to the demand, enterprising men opened inns and taverns. Contact with the outside world stimulated business; merchants learned to draw customers from the surrounding countryside. Northwood became a center of trade.

These are two photographs of the Tasker Inn, where travelers were welcome, and the stage line "Northwood and Epsom Stage Coach" depicts a group of people ready to travel.

Tasker Inn   *Northwood and Epsom Stage Coach*
Source: Borrowed from Gary Tasker's collection of postcards

For many years after the town was settled, many people depended on lumber, which abounded in white pine forests. Mills were built early; the pines were sawn into boards. One of these sawmills was located on the outlet of Jenness Pond. The supply of water from this source was meager, so James decided to increase the flow by having a ditch dug to connect with Long Pond. Instead, a mill pond was created by the additional water, which is now called Little Durgin. The James family ran a sawmill throughout the nineteenth century. In 1900, it was the oldest of any sawmills being operated in Northwood, but it closed soon after that.

James's Sawmill
Source: Borrowed from The Northwood Historical Society

Fortunately, the twentieth century brought unexpected prosperity to Northwood. The lakes, a resource not fully appreciated in early times, attracted summer boarders and then summer residents, who now more than double the off-season population.

The road to Pittsfield and Gilmanton began in the Narrows and ran up over the hill toward Jenness Pond. This road was laid out in 1773, the year the town was incorporated. The crossroads were built at various times as a convenience to residents of the area.

Postcard: 'Two Ways' Northwood Narrow, NH
Source: Borrowed from Gary Tasker's collection of postcards

Northwood has ten lakes or ponds, all partly within its borders. They are: Lucas Pond, North River Pond, Harvey Lake, Pleasant Lake, Northwood Lake, Bow Lake, Little Bow Lake, Durgin Pond, Long Pond, and Jenness Pond.

Postcard: Jenness Pond Road looking down unto Long Pond. #136.
Source: Borrowed from Gary Tasker's collection of postcards

Northwood claims eight of the thirty-six miles of the First New Hampshire Turnpike, now Route 4. In 1973, an estimated five thousand vehicles traveled that highway. Nearly four decades later, it has tripled.

CHAPTER 3

FAMILY TREES

Upon purchasing the cottage I began to look into the history of the area. I purchased the book *A Guide to the History and Old Dwelling Places of Northwood, New Hampshire*, written and complied by Joann Weeks Bailey.

Looking across the James fields and woods you will discover Little Durgin, the pond S. S. James created when he was cultivating wild cranberries and using the excess water from the sawmill. This enterprise, evidently unique in Northwood, proved profitable. Each fall, people were employed to harvest the crop. This pond was named after S. S. James's sister, Abbie James, who married W. M. Durgin. It is given that the hand-dug canal from Long Pond was built to provide water for Durgin Pond, for cranberry growing. This way they could control the flow of water from one pond to the other.

Today, however, due to the development of homes on Long Pond, volunteers control the flow of water. There are no properties built on the shores of this pond; it is owned by the James family. The land is deemed model forest and placed in current use, which means people can use it for fishing, hunting, hiking, cross-country skiing, snowshoeing, and kayaking, but no overnight camping or fire building of any kind. This way the forest is kept as a preserve and the owner gets a tax break.

The telephone transfer installation was once the site of the original James family burying ground. Mr. S. S. James had the bodies moved to the new cemetery that he created, calling it the Fairview Cemetery. This cemetery is high on the hill, which looks out to several small mountains; it is also in back of Johnson's farm. Mr. James took lot 1 for his own family, and the large monument was freighted from Manchester, New Hampshire. James built the wall around the area to resemble the wall surrounding his old homestead.

James Stevens James, son of a sea captain was born in Boston, Massachusetts, on August 25, 1755. In 1780, he married Rebecca Tuttle of Lee. He purchased a large section of undeveloped land in the northwest part of Northwood, near what today is called the Narrows; he cleared the land and built the house. Then, in 1880, the old cape was replaced, and a beautiful Victorian home was constructed on the site. He and Rebecca raised eleven children. Steven James, eldest son of James and Rebecca, worked diligently at farming, clearing more land for pastures. Their fourth child, Samuel James (born April 24, 1788), married Abigail Godfrey in 1810 and had five children. The third child, Samuel Shepherd James (born October 11, 1820), married Martha Hill on January 9, 1845 and raised three daughters and four sons. Samuel purchased his grandfather's farm on April 21, 1850, and continued to still cultivate the land, raise crops, and harvest firewood. The fifth son, Samuel Dudley (born 1855), married Annie B. Hill in 1891 and had two children, Easter and Maurice. They resided mostly in Boston, Massachusetts.

Maurice James and his son Samuel were the last of the James family in Northwood, yet their main residence was in Milwaukee, Wisconsin. Like his grandfather, who was always ready to embrace new concepts, Maurice had made many changes to the homestead. The home was too large for one family, so it was converted to apartments. One of the apartments was set aside to allow living space for himself when he was in town. He enjoyed the Northwood area as a quiet residential place. When he was there, he would oversee his land and supervise the select cutting of trees.

A part of the farm bordering Long Pond was sold to accommodate a private road built along the water's edge. This newly divided area would be called Long Pond Estates. The subdivision plan was approved in June of 1962 by Alder S. Marble and Associates, Registered Engineers and Surveyors, and recorded in the Rockingham County Registry of Deeds.

Being the same premises conveyed to the Grantors by Quitclaim Deed of Long Pond Estates, Inc., dated August 30, 1962, and recorded in Rockingham County Records, Lib. 1640, and Fol. 294.

"Together with the right to pass and repass, in common with others, over a certain right-of-way on land now or formerly of Maurice D. James as described in deed of said James to Long Pond Estates, Inc., dated March 26, 1962, and recorded in the Rockingham County Registry of Deeds, Lib. 1619, Fol. 319".

A private road was built to accommodate the development of Long Pond Estates, Inc. The road passes through a forest of pine and hardwood, which at present is a model forest.

Entrance to Long Pond.

ABSTRACT OF QUITCLAIM DEED

The land conveyed herein is conveyed subject to all flowage and riparian rights, all rights of way and other easements, all zoning and other governmental laws, and regulations and all other provisions of record.

Said land is also conveyed subject to the following provisions:

1. The land conveyed herein shall be used only for residential and camping purposes. No trailers or mobile homes shall be placed or maintained on the land conveyed herein or on any streets or ways shown on the plan first mentioned above.

2. No "For Rent," "For Sale," or other advertising signs or notices shall be place, erected, or maintained on the land conveyed herein without prior written consent of Long Pond Estates, Inc., its successors and assigns; and upon any violation of this provision, the said Long Pond Estates, Inc., its successors and assigns, shall have the right to enter upon the land and to remove such sign or notice.

3. No building, wall, sewerage system, or other structure or installation, or anything used for habitation, shall be erected, placed, constructed, altered or maintained on the land conveyed herein until its plans, specifications, and location on the land have been filed with and approved in writing by said Long Pond Estates, Inc., its successors or assigns. The said Long Pond Estates, Inc., its successors and assigns, shall have the right to refuse to approve any such plans, specifications, and locations which are not suitable or desirable in the exclusive opinion of the said Long Pond Estates, Inc., its successors or assigns. No building shall be located nearer than 25 feet to the shoreline of Long Pond as shown on the plan referred to above, nearer than 20 feet to any roads shown on said plan, or nearer than 6 feet to any other land adjoining the land conveyed herein.

4. No livestock, animals or poultry shall be kept or maintained or allowed on the land conveyed herein, other than household pets.

5. All buildings, structures, installations, and other improvements to be erected, placed, constructed, altered, or maintained on the land conveyed herein must comply with all municipal and other governmental laws, ordinances, by-laws, rules, and regulations duly and validly affecting said land, and if any provision herein differs there from such variance shall not be construed as waiver by the said Long Pond Estates, Inc., of the necessity of compliance with the terms hereof.

6. No noxious, dangerous, offensive, or unduly noise of any nature, nor any activity that may be or become an annoyance or nuisance to owners of other land, shall be permitted on any part of the land conveyed herein.

7. Long Pond Estates, Inc., reserves to itself, its successors and assigns, the right to install, maintain, repair, and replace, under, over, and upon the land conveyed herein and in

8

ways on which said land abuts or abut, such electric light, power, telephone, and telegraph poles and wires; water, sewer, gas, and drainage pipes, mains, and conduits; catch basins, surface drains, and culverts; and such other facilities, installations, appurtenances, and things as the said Long Pond Estates, Inc., its successors and assigns may deem necessary or convenient in connection with the provision of adequate drainage, sewerage disposal, water, gas, electricity, telephone and telegraph communications, and other utilities to any portion of the land conveyed to the said Long Pond Estates, Inc., by said deed of Gerald H. Giles and Ruby Giles, dated March 26, 1962, and recorded in Rockingham County Registry of Deeds, Lib. 1619, Fol. 323, or to any other land heretofore or hereafter conveyed to the said Long Pond Estates, Inc., its successors or assigns, and comprising part of the development of the Long Pond area; and the said Long Pond Estates, Inc., further reserves to itself, its successors and assigns, the right to grant to telephone, telegraph, power, water, and other public and private utility companies and corporations, to municipalities, and to such other persons and corporations as Long Pond Estates, Inc., its successors, and assigns, may determine said right of installation, maintenance, repair, and replacement as above described. Specifically included in the above reservation shall be the right to kill, spray, remove, and trim trees, scrubs, plants, and other growing things in connection with the exercise of the right reserved and the right to provide for flowage of surface and sub-surface drainage onto the land conveyed herein from any land abutting thereon, including streets, ways, and roads. No owner of the land conveyed herein shall in any way obstruct or permit to be obstructed any drainage pipe, main, drain, conduit, culvert, or other type of drainage equipment located on said land, and if any owner shall permit such obstruction to occur and shall fail to take immediate steps to remove such obstruction upon learning thereof he shall be liable to Long Pond Estates, Inc., its successors or assigns in removing the obstruction and for any further expense or damage to which Long Pond Estates, Inc., its successors or assigns may be put as a result of such obstruction and the failure of the owner to remove it.

8. Long Pond Estates, Inc., reserves the right at any time or times to construct and to change the locations, boundaries, courses, and other features of ways shown on any plan on which the land conveyed herein appears or may appear, and to discontinue or abandon entirely any such ways, and to provide ways not previously shown on any plan, so long as the exercise of such right does not deny any land adequate means of access to some public ways.

9. The provisions of paragraphs 1 through 8 above shall run with and bind the land conveyed herein for a period of ninety-nine (99) years from August 30, 1962, and the Long Pond Estates, Inc., its successors and assigns, shall have the right at any time or times during said period to proceed at law or in equity against any person violating or attempting to violate any provisions contained herein, to prevent and abate such violations, to compel compliance with the terms hereof, to enter upon land conveyed

herein and remove any buildings, structures, installations, improvements, or things constructed, erected, installed, or maintained in violation of the terms hereof, at the owners expense and to recover damages or other dues for any violation. Failure to enforce any provision herein contained in any particular instance shall not be deemed a waiver of the right to do so as to any continuing, subsequent, other violation. Long Pond Estates, Inc., reserves to itself, its successors and assigns, the right to use or to permit the use of other land now or in the future owned by said Long Pond Estates, Inc., its successors and assigns, in said Town of Northwood, in a manner at variance with the uses and restrictions provided herein.

10. The grantee or grantees herein, a the case may be, covenant for himself, herself, themselves, or itself and his, her, their, or its theirs, executors, administrators, successors and assigns, that no part of the land surviving of the grantors named prior to twenty (20) after the death of the last surviving of the grantors named herein if there are two or more grantors of the grantor named herein, within first notifying the said Long Pond Estates, Inc., its successors or assigns, in writing of his, her, their, or its intention to convey said land to Long Pond Estates, Inc., its successors or assigns, at the same price and upon the same terms, said offer to be for a period of thirty (30) days. If Long Pond Estates, Inc., its successors, or assigns, shall refuse to accept such offer within said period of thirty (30) days, the grantee or grantees, his, her, their, or its heirs, executors, administrators, successors and assigns shall be free to convey said land, at the price and upon the terms set forth in the above-mentioned notice, for a period of sixty (60) days immediately following the expiration of the thirty (30) day period during which the land was offered to Long Pond Estates, Inc., its successors or assigns. The grantee or grantees, his, her, their, or its heirs, executors, administrators, successors, and assigns, shall not convey said land, or any part thereof, subsequent to said sixty (60) day period without again first notifying Long Pond Estates, Inc., its successors, and assigns in writing, of his, her, their, or its intention to do so, and offering again, in writing, for a period of (30) days, to convey said land to Long Pond Estates, Inc., its successors and assigns, at the same price and on the same terms at which it is intended to be conveyed to any other person, corporation, partnership, or other entity. The obligations of the grantee or grantees, his, her, their, or its heirs, executors, administrators, successors, and assigns set forth in this paragraph are intended as a covenant on their part which shall run with the land for period of twenty (20) years after the death of the grantor named herein, or for a period of twenty (20) years after the death of the last surviving of the grantors named herein if there are two or more grantors named herein. The grantee or grantees further covenants for himself, herself, itself, or themselves, and for his, her, their, or its heirs, executors, administrators, successors and assigns, that for any breach by any of them of any provision of this paragraph they shall be and stand liable to Long Pond Estates, Inc., its successors and assigns, in the amount of one thousand dollars ($1,000.00) as

liquidated damages, or Long Pond Estates, Inc., its successors or assigns, may, at its or their option, compel conveyance to the said Long Pond Estates, Inc., its successors or assigns, of the land involved, at the same price and other terms at which the grantee or grantees, his, her, their, or its heirs, executors, administrators, successors, or assigns attempted to convey the land to any other person, corporation, partnership, or other entity.

11. It is further provided that each lot included in this conveyance shall be subject to an annual charge of thirty-six dollars ($36.00) and the grantee or grantees, his, her, their, or its heirs, executors, administrators, successors, and assigns hereby agree:

    a.   To pay annually to Long Pond Estates, Inc., its successors or assigns, the sum of $36.00 for each lot hereby conveyed, on or before the first day of May of each year hereafter, for the right to enjoy such of the following privileges, facilities, improvements, service, and benefits as Long Pond Estates, Inc., its successors or assigns, in its or their absolute discretion, may from time to time provide for the use and benefit of persons who pay said annual charge of $36.00 and who own any of the land conveyed to Long Pond Estates, Inc., by deed of Gerald H. Giles and Ruby M Giles, dated March 26, 1962, and recorded with Rockingham County Registry of Deeds in Book 1619, Page 323.

        i.   Recreational privileges and facilities.

        ii.   Land improvement, and the purchase, construction, alteration, and maintenance of buildings, dams, and other forms of property.

        iii.   Payment of taxes and assessments levied by the Town of Northwood or any other public authority on any land or other property used for the general use of benefit of such owners.

        iv.   Construction, improvement, drainage, and maintenance of roads, streets, and travel ways.

        v.   Miscellaneous services and benefits, including without limiting the generality of the foregoing insect control, police services, and utilities.

    b.   That the use of such privileges, facilities, improvements, services and benefits shall be subject to approval of the user for membership in Long Pond Landowner's Association and compliance with the rules and regulations from time to time promulgated by Long Pond Estates, Inc., its successors and assigns with respect to such use, and that the said Long Pond Estates, Inc., its successors and assigns, shall have the right to deny to the grantee or grantees, his, her, their, or its heirs, executors, administrators, successors, and assigns, the use and enjoyment of said privileges, facilities, improvements, service, and benefits for violation of such rules and regulations, without impairing the obligation to pay the charge as herein set forth.

c. The said charge shall constitute a debt which may be collected by suit or action in any court of competent jurisdiction, and that said charge shall constitute a lien or encumbrance on the land conveyed herein until paid.

d. The acceptance of this deed shall construed to be a covenant on the part of the grantee or grantees, his, her, their, or its heirs, executors, administrators, successors, and assigns, to pay said charge as provided herein, and that upon conveyance of any of the land herein described, each successive owner thereof shall from the time of acquiring title be held to have covenanted and agreed to pay Long Pond Estates, Inc., its successors or assigns, this charge.

e. That this charge shall run with and bind the land herein conveyed and shall be binding upon the grantee or grantees, his, her, their, or its heirs, executors, administrators, successors, and assigns, until December 31, 1982, unless earlier terminated by written release of Long Pond Estates, Inc., its successors and assigns.

f. The lien hereby reserved and described shall, however, be at all times subordinate to the lien of any of any bona fide mortgage of any of the land herein conveyed, to the end and intent that the lien of any such mortgage shall be paramount to the lien for the charge herein imposed and provided further, that such subordination shall apply only to the charges that shall become payable prior to the passing of title under foreclosure of such mortgage or acquisition of title by deed in lieu of foreclosure; and nothing contained shall be held to affect the rights herein given to enforce the collection of such charges accruing after foreclosure of such mortgage by sale or otherwise, or after conveyance in lieu of foreclosure.

CHAPTER 4

INTERVIEW WITH
AUDREY HUCKINS

In 2003, I sat with Audrey as she related to me the story of how things seem to happen on the Long Pond area. She was one of the first to settle in one of the lots. Lot 131 is one of the first areas of land you see as you turn onto the lake road. She purchased a lot directly across the road to build a garage for her automobile. She and her first husband tented on the land. They built a bungalow-style cottage, but their unhappy marriage resulted in a divorce and disagreements over the land and buildings on the lake and the property in the city of Portsmouth, New Hampshire. She obtained the lake home for her two boys and herself. It mysteriously burnt on Thanksgiving Day, 1969, while she and her second husband were away on their honeymoon. They rebuilt right away in 1970; it was completed as a split-level home.

The road was completed up to the Y and then up over the hill to the right side to make a turnaround, as the property line ended there. Bob Bailey did the plowing, but only to the split in the road. Bob purchased an area of land and lived across the lake. Ed Shinn was actually the first to build on this site, at the end of the road. He built in such a way that it took on the appearance of a bomb shelter. He did build a house on it, but kids destroyed the house. He then had to rebuild, but he retained the appearance of an underground home.

The lots at that time sold for two hundred dollars. Ed Shinn decided to purchase many of the land lots. Audrey believed he may have purchased six or seven. Jay Blier also purchased six or more lots for the same price, as the developer wanted to rid himself of this development.

The model cottage was built about halfway down the road, facing the public beach area. The style and design of the model was called an A-frame. Salvatore and Josephine Aiello of Everett, Massachusetts, and John and Anna Chutes of Francestown, New Hampshire, were among the first people to have the A-frame constructed on their lots.

Bob Bailey acquired several lots from the developer in exchange for doing work, as well as bringing in gravel, rocks, and sand. The developer wanted the front of lot 17 filled with sand so it could be advertised and used as a public launch for the campers, especially the back lots, which had no access to the pond. He worked one day bringing in load after load of sand for the public landing, but when he returned the next day, it all seemed to have disappeared. They then measured the depth of water in front of the area—sixty feet. Needless to say, he stopped that process.

Mr. and Mrs. Bailey were having their fifth child and needed extra money, so he sold one of the lots he acquired. Two weeks later it was sold again, for seven thousand dollars, to Joseph Grady, who was Audrey's brother-in-law. They made a profit, but Joseph was also very enterprising. His first purchase was further up the road on a hill, which he purchased for one dollar. He didn't build; he just camped on it. Then he sold it. Audrey did not know the price, but she felt he made a profit.

Rita McKay from Saugus, Massachusetts, was also one of the first people to purchase a cottage from the developer. This cottage was different from the A-frame style. Most cottages built in this style had two bedrooms and an open family area with kitchen space.

Audrey also related to me how the Introduction to the Forming of the Long Pond Property Owners, Northwood, New Hampshire, came about. I looked into this and obtained a copy of the first recorded minutes for the formation of the association.

CHAPTER 5

BIRTH OF THE
LONG POND ASSOCIATION

MINUTES OF MEETING, AUGUST 19, 1972 (copied exactly as reported)

As of August 19, 1972, a meeting was held at Mr. and Mrs. Al Huckins backyard, it was brought to order at 1:20 p.m. by President Richard Sears. At this time it was stated that Long Pond Estates, Inc., sent a letter dated September 20, 1972, to each owner stating they no long are responsible to maintain the road and beaches. With this meeting the "Long Pond Property Owners of Northwood, New Hampshire," was officially formed. The lawyers were Dudley & Sanderson of Portsmouth, New Hampshire. They will deal with Mr. Dudley of Durham, New Hampshire. For filing purposes our incorporators are Al & Audrey Huckins, Bud Bates, Joe Grady, Ed Shinn, Dick Sears, Earl & Alice Newkirk, and Russ Eldridge; the legal address is 7 Lake Drive, Long Pond, Northwood, New Hampshire, 03261.

The articles of the by-laws were read off. Long Pond Property Owners of Northwood, New Hampshire

1. Designation of powers of corporation;
2. Dissolution of corporation, etc.

The purpose of the organization is to substitute Long Pond Property Owners of Northwood, New Hampshire, for Long Pond Estates, Inc., which had lost interest in sustaining roads, beaches, and is more than willing to deed over their rights to us. A copy of this transfer is being reviewed by our lawyers now—the basic transfer being:

1. A 30' right-of-way over private property from East Jenness Pond Road into Lake Drive.
2. All roads within area (Lake Drive, Sunset Point, and Lookout Point).

3. Boat landing (lot 17) and beach (lot 43) this land not being taxed by the town.
4. Collection of $36.00 annually until 1982, when association may continue or increase as voted on at that time.

Decision was made by those present to have an annual meeting on the first Saturday after July 4. Discussion was held regarding number for a quorum. It was decided to let the lawyer determine the number. It was felt that all important policy matters should be voted on by members either by attendance or by proxy. However, decided that at least ten members should be present to hold an official meeting. It was noted that a notice will be sent out ten days before any future meeting and will list business to be covered. Policy matters of substance will be handled at annual meetings.

The officers are to be: President, Vice President, Treasurer, and a clerk. These are to hold offices for at least one year and until new officers are elected.

President Sears also stated that the by-laws were kept as general as possible to cover us under the law. Amendments may be made later as a need arises. A copy of these laws will be given to each member.

It was noted that the road was repaired this year for the first time in years. It was graded in June and filled and leveled in July and August. Our thanks is given to Ed Shinn and Dick Sears.

FINANCES: The treasurer's report was given by Treasurer Russ Eldridge.

Dues have been collected from 25 members with 39 property owners still unpaid, five who are using the roads and beach area (Dow, Philbrick, Roux, D'Eon, and Soles).

There is a collection of $900.00 to date with interest of $3.18 for a total of $903.18.

Have paid bills of: Bailey (road work) $400.00, title passing $1.00, NH Corporation Filing Fee $10.00, miscellaneous $2.00, total expenses $413.00.

Have $490 left to pay lawyers fee of $50-$100 plus snow-plowing charges and sign preparation.*

*Note: As of 10/13/72, have received $36 from D'Eon and $36 to be received from Long Pond Estates (lot 77), plus interest $8.50 and expenses of $90 for legal and $25 for the sign. Total in bank plus amount due from Long Pond Estates, Inc., now totals $455.68.

Discussed how to collect from those not paying. Should interest be charged on overdue dues or should we just embarrass them if they are using facilities? No notices have been sent out by treasurer until actual transfer has taken place. Also noted that original corp. will transfer any dues paid to them this year. (Would not show books at the time of meeting with them as we had not formed a legal association.)

DISCUSSIONS: Ed Shinn thanked R. Eldridge and Dick Sears and others involved for time spent in forming the association. Then he proposed that we sign a petition asking for appropriation of money to plow our roads. As we pay $4,000 in taxes and get no return on our money, he felt that they should at least help us in this way. This petition should be presented to select men by December for them to review it and then warrant can be drawn for April town meeting. Annex New Hampshire town selectman Bob Hotchkiss said it was too late to get money for plowing or anything this year. He also stated that we would be better off petitioning for road repair aid rather than plowing as right-of-way being only 30' was 10' too small for town to ever take over the road. However, they may help us on a 50' basis on the care of the road if the petition is made into warrant and passed at the April town meeting. A petition was signed by those present, asking for road repair aid in return for our taxes paid.

ZONING: The changed zoning code was mentioned as this may hinder single-lot owners from building. However, as land was subdivided in 1961 and 1962 an individual may have a better chance of getting a variance. (All subject to state acceptable sewerage facilities.) This will be who question regulations. Checked into so that the association will better be able to advise single-lot owners or others

COLLECTIONS OF DUES: Noted that transfer of property cannot take place until past dues are collected. If any owners default land for back taxes, loss of interest if dues exceed value of land, we should (association) list such property so that any members who wish additional land will be able to buy—the corporation itself doesn't want more land.

VANDALISM: Ira Levy mentioned the fact that he had had much vandalism in past four years. He wondered about police protection. Was told the police (state) are seen patrolling from time to time. As more people have homes and live here year round, it was felt that fewer strangers will be around and vandalism should subside.

PUBLIC BEACH: Al Dyer wanted assurance as a back-lot owner that work would be done next year for certain. He feels his dues are wasted, as he is only here for two months in summer. He has little concern for snow plowing (money saved for that and if lots of snow, none would be left for beach work). Was noted that thanks to Newkirks, some sand was given and leveling done. Need boulders and stumps removed then sand to fill areas. Al Dyer was assured work will be done on the beach next year. Also an informal work group will get together to cut brush and do whatever possible to make the beach better. Boat ramp can't be taken care of as water level has to be way down in order to fix washout.

ROAD CARE & PLOWING: It was decided to get at least three competitive prices before a contract be given out. It was also decided that both roads and beach work would be cheaper if done at the same time by same firm. Plowing will be checked on also for this winter. Probably will be charged by the storm, but we will pay these bills monthly so as to keep accounts clear. Another work group will be gathered to cut brush at sides of the road to alleviate blind spots. Culverts should be shored up with logs and passing areas cleared. It was stressed that speed should be cut down. A sign voted upon to be located at entrance of road (all name signs to be removed and may be picked up at Huckins home). The sign should read something to the effect of, "Long Pond—private way—patrolled—drive slowly." The price of such a sign is being checked on by Ed Shinn. It was voted that $25 be the maximum we would pay. A sign for Lake Drive giving names and lot (directory) is desired in near future.

Road work is planned for spring as soon as water level has subsided. As dues are due April 1 (billed in March) money should be in to complete this work. Also have hopes in future of having town road agent oil roads when is oiling. Hoping that road aid is granted to us by the town fathers, at the April town meeting of 1973. Do hope roads won't be used unless absolutely necessary during wet spring period. Spraying for mosquitoes was questioned and will have that checked on at a later time with state pest control. The meeting was adjourned at 3:00 p.m.

Respectfully submitted,
Jo Eldridge, Acting Clerk

Members present at the first meeting, August 19, 1972, of Long Pond Property Owners of Northwood, New Hampshire were: Dick Sears, Al & Audrey Huckins, Ed Shinn, Bud & Joanne Bates, Earl & Alice Newkirk, Carl & Eileen Golden, Al Dyer, Bob & Helen Hotchkiss, Russ & Jo Eldridge, Charlie & Coretta McCann, Ira Levy, and Jay Blier.

The following letter from Gould H. Coleman, Treasurer, Long Pond Estates, Inc., 470 Main Street, fifth floor, Fitchburg, Massachusetts, 01420, dated September 20, 1972, states the new association (Long Pond Estates) will take on all responsibilities.

Dear Long Pond lot owners:

Paragraph numbered 11 of your sales contract with Long Pond Estates, Inc. (and paragraph number 11 of your deed to your land at Long Pond Estates, if you have already been deeded that land) requires you to pay an annual charge of $36.00 to Long Pond Estates, Inc., in order that the roads will be maintained and plowed, the beach area kept up, etc.

This is to inform you that Long Pond Estates, Inc., has transferred and assigned the right to collect the $36.00 annual charge to a newly organized association of lot owners at Long Pond Estates, Inc., called "Long Pond Property Owners of Northwood, New Hampshire." This means the Association has full power to collect the annual charge from you exactly as provided in your sales contract and deed. Long Pond Estates, Inc., no longer has anything to do with the annual charge.

The new Association has taken on all responsibilities in connection with the roads, beaches, etc., and it is hoped that you will want to take an active interest in the affairs of this Association along with all other lot owners at Long Pond Estates.

Signed by Gould H Coleman,
Treasurer,
Long Pond Estates, Inc. 470 Main Street,
fifth floor, Fitchburg, Massachusetts

Louis C. Wyman, on December 8, 1973, sent a letter stating the town would not provide any maintenance regarding the Long Pond Road, leaving it totally up to the lot owners. This was issued by Rockingham County SS E-1961-73, Superior Court, September Term, 1973.

CHAPTER 6

RECREATIONAL CRAFTS

At the 1986 annual meeting a possible development across the pond was discussed. People believed this would cause overcrowding and use of motorboats and jet skis. Therefore a committee was formed to study the project.

At the 1987 annual meeting of Long Pond owners, a motion was passed to request Senator Johnson to introduce legislation to limit to 10 HP the use of motors on Long Pond, with a grandfather clause: those owners who had motorboats on Long Pond in 1987 might continue using them for five more years.

The scare was a result of a rumor that a developer had purchased the large lot of land across the body of water and would be building several houses with water rights. So several people proceeded to get together and pass a petition around for a few to sign. Then the petition was presented to State Senator Johnson, who lived in Northwood, on Northwood Lake. State Senator William Johnson of District 17 (representative of Rockingham District 17) presented the bill to the 1988 session. It was Senate Bill No. 245. Three years after this bill had passed, no building or increase in motor traffic on the pond occurred, so several landowners formed a committee to oppose it. Five families, mine among them, met at the statehouse asking to revisit the bill 245. We went before the panel at the state house to voice our opinions and concerns.

As the spokesperson, I introduced the following letter and message:

I would like to step back into the history of this bill (1986), when Mr. Golden (who was living in New York and came to New Hampshire for the summer and was therefore not a permanent resident) proceeded to get a few others together about their concerns:

1. Large boats would harm the loons.
2. Large boats caused waves that would erode the shoreline.
3. The big concern was a developer. They heard that condos were going to be built across the water and feared this would bring more motorboats.

Because of these concerns, several met with Senator Johnson, but they forgot about the people who opposed this. The wildlife was not hurt by the boats. The erosion of the shore was false because large rocks are in front of most of the cottages, and boats stay at least 250 feet away from the shoreline. As far as the rumor of the condo building—it was false (I went to the planning board to check and nothing purposed), so why worry?

At the next annual meeting, July 9, 1987, twenty-two members showed up, and it was voted 16 to 22 to wait and see. But Mr. Golden and his committee did not wait. Instead, it put through as Bill RSA 48634. When the hearing came up, only a few knew about it and so no one was there to oppose it. Had only one of the families who currently owned a motorboat been there, they would have defended their rights and the rights of the other three owners. We appreciated the grandfather clause of five years of use, but the time is up and nothing has changed on the body of water. So we are asking for another four years or for the whole cause to be thrown out.

There are still only three families using motorboats: Janusius, owned thirty-seven years; Bates, owned over twenty years; and DuPonts, owned seventeen years. We have never had an accident, always wear proper safety equipment, and always stay away from people and other boasts. We have never landed on any other property but our own.

I had spoken to Mr. and Mrs. Russell Eldridge, who supported the bill, but he presently feels he shouldn't have, because his family also enjoys the ski boating. People who see no problem to having the motorboats are: Mr. and Mrs. J. Belanger, Mr. and Mrs. McKay, Mr. and Mrs. Hotchkiss, Mr. and Mrs. O'Donnell, Mr. Faulkner, Mr. and Mrs. Bates, Mr. and Mrs. J. Chutes, and several others.

There is no public access, so the public cannot bring their boats into Long Pond; thus the boating is limited only to residents of Long Pond.

After all the discussion and speeches pro and con, we were all dismissed.

We heard several weeks later the restrictions regarding boating on Long Pond were removed, and any resident was able to use their motorboats and water-ski.

No sooner had the boating rules been revisited and motorboats had again been allowed to float on Long Pond than the issue of Jet Skis came to light. Several people met together and submitted a petition to restrict the use of Jet Skis on Long Pond. The petition to restrict the use of Jet Skis was mailed July 19, 1989, to the commissioner of safety. The letter regarding Jet Ski craft on Long Pond was submitted by Preston F. Marshall on August 11, 1989. We sent an opposing letter August 25, 1989. With this, a hearing was scheduled and the hall was packed.

See the copy of newspaper article from the *Concord Monitor,* Saturday August 26, 1989. The findings, rulings, and order RSA 48634 for the original bill was revised and the commissioner found no basis to limit or restrict the use of craft on Long Pond pursuant to RSA 270:75.

Big Feud On Long Pond

Jet Ski Backers Pack Northwood Hearing

By FELICE BELMAN
Monitor Staff Writer

NORTHWOOD — Irene DuPont and Preston Marshall are neighbors on Long Pond. In July, they even served on a two-person lake committee together. But last night, as they waited for a meeting to start at the Northwood Town Hall, DuPont and Marshall and their families stood on opposite sides of the parking lot. They didn't speak.

The meeting was about jet skis. DuPont has one, and Marshall wants them banned from Long Pond. The disagreement — like jet ski disputes all across the state this summer — attracted a roomful of lakeside residents, a hearing officer from the Department of Safety and a marine patrol officer.

Tom Cunningham, the hearing officer, had already been to two jet ski hearings. He laid out the ground rules patiently and cautioned the testifiers not to get too emotional or to speak for too long. That didn't always work.

Most of the testimony was in favor of jet skis, and some of it was dramatic. The speakers said there had never been any complaints about jet skis on Long Pond, so there was no reason to ban them now.

"If there's no problem, then why eliminate our jet ski?" asked DuPont. "Why go on chemotherapy if you don't have cancer? Why go on a diet if you're not fat?"

And John Bell, who also rides a jet ski on Long Pond, said: "First it's the jet ski, then it'll be the boats. What about the motorcycles everybody loves to ride? I thought this was New Hampshire and live free or die."

Gary Tasker said he and his family had had a jet ski on Long Pond longer than some of their opponents had lived there.

To Marshall, however, it was simply a matter of space. He had initiated the hearing by sending a pe-

See JET SKIS — Page 12

DAN HABIB/Monitor Staff

(Left to right) Gary Tasker, Roxanne DuPont, Jennifer DuPont, Irene DuPont and Paul DuPont put their feelings in writing by their home.

Newspaper Article, Concord Monitor, NH

This body of water is enjoyed by everyone in so many different ways; these photographs capture a few of the various methods the residences enjoy water sports.

Collage of boats on Long Pond

CHAPTER 7

BUSINESS OF THE ROAD

As of the beginning (1972) of the Long Pond Estates, Inc., the dues were thirty-six dollars a year to pay for the road repairs, plowing, and maintaining the beach area. As of August 17, 1991, the dues were set at the rate of $125 a year to maintain the roadway and beaches. This was voted on for five years, and at the end of that time, it would be revisited. Mr. W. Faulkner sent a letter to the Town of Northwood regarding the taxes on the beaches and roads of Long Pond, asking for an abatement of taxes. It was answered July 15, 1997, by stating they would allocate the valuation placed on the roads and breaches to all the properties within the Long Pond Estates, beginning with the first 1997 tax bill. This will result in each property owner receiving a slightly higher assessment, but it will be shared by all.

In the year of 2007-2008, the association fee had been voted in to be $375 per year, for the road and the replacement of the culvert caused the budget to grow. This road had been plowed, graded, and filled whenever it was needed. As of the meeting on July 14, 2012, the board plans on reviewing the dues—not to raise the dues, but perhaps drop it down a little, as there is a large sum of money in the bank, and it would help everyone's budget. According to people living in other surrounding areas that have dirt roads, ours at Long Pond is maintained as one of the best.

Street Numbering (effective March 31, 1995) by the Board of Selectmen NH RSA 231:133-a. This was to provide a means for expedient of emergency response by fire, police, rescue, and other emergency services. Long Pond Estates was assigned numbers, and the Long Pond Road was divided up with Bates Landing and Lookout Point. All numbers must be made visible for all to see.

Small Business Issue

The opening of a small business endeavor by a landowner was called forth by the Long Pond board to investigate this issue. Letters sent to property owners on March 19, 2000, regarding the specialist gun shop at 202 Long Pond Road. He was seeking the approval of a small business in his home. The petition was placed before the Northwood Planning Board to collect and sell firearms. There would be no advertising on the land. According to the rules of the Long Pond Property Owners quitclaim deed, Provision 1 states this area is to be used only for residential property. A planning board meeting was held May 25, 2000, in Northwood Town Hall to discuss this proposal. The decision was made on July 8, 2000, by the board to keep the covenant/quitclaim deed that prohibits retail business of any kind on that road. The business owner was very upset regarding this decision, but overall the residents were pleased, as this area is a small community of wonderful people.

CHAPTER 8

WRITTEN ACCOUNTS
OF LANDOWNERS

This shows the architectural layout of the Long Pond area.

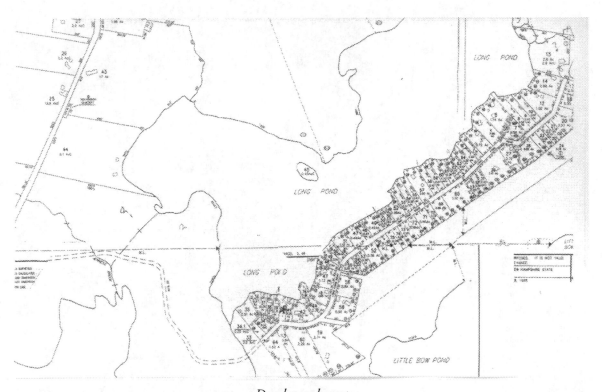

Developers layout
Source: Northwood Tax Office

I have listed some of the owners and transfers of properties across the pond and within the shoreline of Long Pond, telling some folklore and stories as I know, from people, incidents, and experiences. Some have the assessor's map number, lot number, or road number for fire purposes; not all are complete.

The photograph shows a statue of a blue heron, which one can see flying around the pond as well as standing in the tall grasses found in the coves all summer long.

A friend on the pond—blue heron.

Dean MacFarland, Lots 36, 37, 38, and 45

The land across from the Long Pond Estates properties is in current use; therefore, hunting is allowed. This terrain covers approximately one-third of the shoreline, including 4,446 feet of waterfront. A beautiful home was built upon the land, but it is far enough off the shoreline that it is partly hidden. A small pier was constructed on the shore to allow a person to launch a boat, but to date it is not a busy area.

Louise Welch, Lot 43
178 Jenness Pond Road
Northwood, New Hampshire 03261

Louise Welch's property is directly across from one-third of the Long Pond Estates property. She has approximately 513 feet of waterfront. In earlier years there was a cottage on the shoreline, but it was burnt down at the owner's request. At the present time, there is nothing on the beach except a dock with a few boats. The original farmhouse was moved down route 107 to another piece of land, allowing space for a new home to be built.

The beautiful view seen across the pond in the winter

Phillip Janusis, Lot 44
24 Janusis Lane
Northwood, New Hampshire 03261

These are original homes built many years ago, and have about 790 feet of water frontage.

The oldest homes on the Pond

This land abuts the James model forest available for current use. There is a runoff stream from Jenness Pond that runs under the dirt road to the model forest area. Due to the heavy flow of water, a drain was placed under the road, allowing it to flow into Little Durgins.

The following photograph was taken during the spring season of 2008. Due to heavy rain for many days, flooding occurred at this low area in the road. The water became so deep that boats were left on one side, while their automobiles had to be parked on the other side of the road. Since that time, that section of the road has been built up in hopes it will never flood again.

Road closed
Source: Photograph by Michael Travis, August 3, 2008

Vincent and Joanne Bates
44 Jenkins Road
Andover, Massachusetts 01810

In 1992, Mr. and Mrs. Bates purchased lot 35 from Alphonse and Marie Gerrato of Portsmouth, New Hampshire, who had originally purchased it from the developer.

Lot 2 (36)

This waterfront lot was purchased from John and Jean Lane of Northwood, New Hampshire, in 1969. The Lanes had purchased it from Long Pond Estates in 1962. The Bates eventually built a garage on the lot.

Lot 3 (37)

This waterfront lot and cottage was purchased in 1969 from John and Florence Better, Jr., of Marshfield, Massachusetts, who had purchased it from the Long Pond Estates in 1962.

Lot 4 (38 and 34.1, 34)

This waterfront lot and cottage, as well as two back lots, were purchased from Richard and Muriel Sears of Hooksett, New Hampshire, in 1974. They purchased it from Leo and Angele Tardif in 1968. In 1976, Mr. and Mrs. Bud Bates sold the house on this waterfront to her father, Vito Mensale, and his wife. Upon the death of Mr. Vito Mensale, it was returned to the Bates family, which consisted of two sisters and a bother. Then, in 2003, Joanne Bates became the sole owner.

Gary and Kim Bates, Lots 5 and 39
52 Martel Road
Chichester, New Hampshire 03234

This lot was originally owned by Arthur Modis, but then Richard Batchelder purchased it in 1969. He had a large family, consisting of ten children, and came from the Hampton area. In 1975, Lil Sunderland purchased this property; she came from Dover, New Hampshire, and had five children. Jack Houlihan purchased the property from her, but he passed away in 2000, leaving the property for sale.

Gary Bates, the son of Mr. and Mrs. Vincent Bates purchased the property in 2001. The Bates family proceeded to do a lot of improvements on their property, digging it out and placing it on a foundation, to improve the value of it. Vincent and Gary Bates are the caretakers of the water level and also serve as the beaver dam controllers. When one of the heavy windstorms hit the Long Pond area, a big pine tree fell into the canal area, nearly filling the passageway. When Gary saw this, he and several other friends, using chainsaws and ropes, removed the tree from the waterway. Their efforts proved to be quite significant. By acting quickly, they prevented any possible problems with the flow and drainage of the canal from developing.

In 2009, a microburst occurred at the Long Pond Area. Several large trees came down but never touched the houses. Mrs. Bates was in the upstairs bedroom when this occurred, and fortunately she never realized how close the tree branches had come to crashing through the roof where she was standing.

Several years earlier, in the area of the Bates residence, my husband and friends were down by the water; it became quite windy. A giant gust of wind moved across the water in such a way that the water picked up momentum and spun around, creating a waterspout. Some of the storms in this area can be very violent because of the layout of the land and water. Fortunately, on this particular occasion, no damage resulted! This little island is difficult to approach or land on, due to the pond lilies and vegetation surrounding it.

When 911 service was established, all the roads had to have addresses that could be easily found, so a few changes had to occur. Sunset Drive, for example, was too close to Sunset Way. Russ Eldridge, a clever soul, took the liberty of calling the road Bates Lane.

Bates Lane

Thomas and Lorraine Horne, Lots 6 and 63
129 Long Pond Road

Tom and Lorraine Horne of Nashua, New Hampshire, had owned lot 78, at Long Pond and sold it. Then they decided to purchase this piece of property from Carolyn Herbert-Shaw. After buying it, they renovated the cottage and enhanced the grounds with a cobblestone patio. In addition, this property included a lot of land across the road. This lot is approximately 60 feet by 617.8 feet deep. They are presently in the process of creating a road to gain access to the high-hill area, where they may someday build a home.

Barbara Hamm
Bates Lane

The wide expanse of land surrounding the ponds of Little Bow and Durgin, up and through the power lines to the Victorian house on the main road as well as five rights-of-way to enter the land, was owned by Maurice D. James until his death. Now it is owned by his daughter, Barbara Hamm, from Mequon, Wisconsin. This land is an established model forest, run by a hired forester, who authorizes logging every so many years to keep the forest healthy. This allows the public to use the forest and deems the property in current use; therefore, the owner receives a tax deduction.

Audrey Huckins, Lots 7, 64, 65, and 66
131 Long Pond Road

When Audrey and her first husband purchased the waterfront lot, they would come and tent on the land. Then, as time went on, they built a small bungalow. Due to black-fly season, they soon added an eight-by-ten-foot screened room. After they divorced in 1969, Audrey decided to keep the Long Pond property, where a new split level home was soon built. In this home she raised two boys, John and Steven, who grew up in and around the woods and pond of Northwood. In fact, they became among the first year-round people living on the pond. They decided to have a two-stall garage built across the road from their dwelling place.

What was left after the fire   *Audrey Huckins and son*
in front of her home

Source: Polaroid by Audrey Huckins

Larry and Kristal Huppe, Lots 8 and 9
135 Long Pond Road

    This two-story home, including a two-stall garage on a separate lot, was originally owned by Charles and Loretta McCann; they resided there for many years. After Charlie's passing, Loretta lived there until she was placed in assisted living. She did not drive, so she had to depend on others to get to where she had to go. But while Charlie was alive, he proved to be quite a character; he always had a good word for everyone and could tell a good joke or come up with a clever line to make someone laugh. This home is now owned by Larry and Kristal Huppe. Larry has served the association as road agent for many years. He is a good neighbor who has assisted anyone with problems in so many ways. His property is level with the pond, making it very easy to launch boats, but due to the odd shape of his land, he has little shoreline. He also owns a pontoon boat, which he greatly enjoys. He likes pulling the children around in a tube or just giving rides to friends and neighbors. No matter what he is doing, he always has his dog, Midnight, with him.

Diane and Ernest Davey, Lots 67, 68, and 69
142 Long Pond Road

A stranger, unknown to residents, went in and cut all the trees and cleared the land on these lots. Then, in 1986, on this parcel of land, a little log house was built. Joseph Farvalero purchased it and moved in. For many years, he was the road agent for the association. He sold the property on August 11, 2002, to Michael Meserve and Debra Nichols. This home is very cute and friendly; it has sliding glass doors that exit onto a beautiful patio with an in-ground pool. This dwelling is not built near a shoreline and is set back off the road with a slightly curved driveway, allowing for a great deal of privacy. On one small corner of the land, there is a section that abuts the body of water known as Little Bow.

Aerial view of Long Pond shoreline and Little Bow
Source: Photograph by Gary Tasker

This pond has only a few access roads to it. They are roadways owned by Maurice James's daughter, Barbara Hamm. No homes are built on the property surrounding the water. However, the State of New Hampshire Fish and Game has used it several times to restock other ponds with bass. They would come in and launch two boats. One boat would have an electric charge with prongs that they would insert into the water. By sending an electric charge into the water, the fish would rise. The other boat would net the fish they desired and place them in a holding tank. Then they would transfer these fish to another lake or pond. I don't believe they do this anymore, as we haven't seen this activity for a long time.

Before the homes were built on this property, including lots 67, 68, and 69, many fishermen would follow a path through the woods to a point where they could fish from shore or launch a rowboat. Now that axis has been voided and a home built, making it difficult to get a clear and easy path to the shoreline, and even though there is still a right-of-way to get to the pond, most of the year the trail is very marshy and difficult to walk through without going up to one's knees in mud. This pond is also good for duck hunting. Many species of ducks do land and feed in these grassy areas. When winter comes, many people walk in through the frozen marsh area to ice fish, snowshoe, cross-country ski, or ride snowmobiles. In fact, the snowmobile club in this town maintains a trail through that forest area, and one trail goes to the Lake Shore Farm Inn, situated on Jenness Pond's shoreline.

Paul and Irene DuPont, John and Anna Chute, and their relatives and friends, would ride that whole area from Long Pond, Little Bow, Big Bow, and Jenness Pond, up through the power lines with their snow machines. Sometimes they would end up at Lake Shore Farms to have a hot cup of coffee and a great meal. Those were wonderful times and great experiences to savor.

Lake Shore Farms always welcomes snowmobilers, and in the summer they typically hold rallies. These rallies offered snowmobilers the opportunity to race across the small pond (which is a water hole on their land across the street from the inn), and the contestants would try to make it to the other side. Of course, many fail in this attempt and end up in the water, commonly called "the drink." To pull the machine out of the pond, a man wearing a wetsuit goes in and hooks the machine to a winch to extricate it from the water. This is a way of raising money for the club and the inn.

In 1990, after the rally was over and most were cleaning up and heading out, the barn of Lake Shore Farm suddenly burst into flames. This created a dilemma for the fire department as they rushed to get there and save the inn. The barn was totaled and the inn's second floor was damaged. In time, the barn was rebuilt and the inn was restored to full use again.

Snowmobiling over the watering hole

The remains of the burnt barn and inn.

The inn was always a favorite place for visitors coming in from all around the east coast, to stay and enjoy the Jenness Pond Shore. This inn was owned by Ellis and Eloise Ring in the early 1900s, but since their death, it has been in financial trouble and at the time of this writing, is presently up for sale.

Enjoy Lake Shore Inn, Northwood, NH.
Source: Borrowed from Gary Tasker's collection of postcards

Stephanie Buzzell, Lots 70, 71, and 72
150 Long Pond Road

Jay Blier purchased many lots from the developer for two hundred dollars each when the company decided to remove themselves from this project; among these were lots 70, 71, and 72. He was not the only one who jumped at this opportunity. In 1986, Stephanie Buzzell purchased these three lots from the Bliers and submitted plans to build. After those plans were approved, some land was cleared and a two-bedroom home was built on the lots. It is set back from the road and has a curved driveway that turns into an attached garage. It is a beautiful house with great landscaping that enhances the property. Stephanie, who is a kind-hearted soul, allows fishermen to park to the side of her driveway in order to enter the Little Bow Pond to fish. This is especially thoughtful on her part because the access has no parking facilities.

Kathleen Stapleton, Lot 10
151 Long Pond Road

This camp was one of the original places built by the developer as a model. It is owned by Rita McKay of Saugus, Massachusetts; she has a grandson, Shawn, who loved to fish, swim, and boat in the waters of Long Pond. He is about the same age as my son, Billy, and the boys became friends. When Rita passed away, the property was transferred to Kathleen Stapleton of Saugus, Massachusetts.

A small, fifteen-foot section of this property was filled in by leaves and debris over a period of years, creating what is now a peninsula. Today it has become part of the mainland, and on the tax map it is listed as lot number 76 and is owned by no one.

Although this transformation occurred over time, it now creates a different water flow, which produces a problem for the neighbors, who believe that this water flow causes lilies to grow near the shore area. Furthermore, it also cuts down the shoreline of the two abutting homeowners of lots 42 and 46.

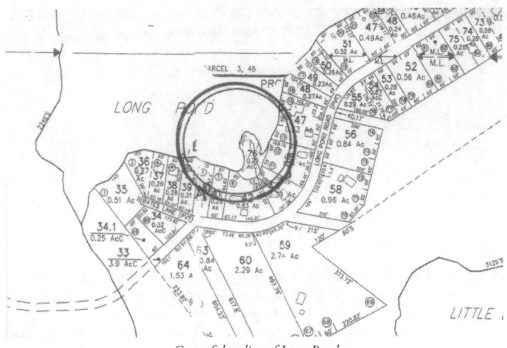

Copy of shoreline of Long Pond
Source: the Northwood town tax office

Michael Travis, Lots 11 and 12
157 Long Pond Road

Lot 11 was owned by Steven and Cathy Henson of Portsmouth, New Hampshire, and lot 12 was first owned by Peter and Lisa Swenson, of Concord, New Hampshire. It was sold to Joseph and Rita Belanger of Manchester, New Hampshire. Joseph built the camp on this lot. It is a cute little cottage, but it was constructed very close to the ground; as a result, it did not allow any space to add insulation, and the cottage was difficult to heat.

Later, when the house was purchased by Michael Travis, changes needed to be made. After buying it in the late fall, he tried to live there during the winter months, but he nearly froze during the first cold snap. He explained how he moved into one area and hunkered down in that spot to endure the ferocious, cold temperatures and wait the winter out.

Since the purchase, Michael has done a tremendous amount of rebuilding, up and down and out the back. Purchasing lot 11 added to the size of his property. The place now has a wonderful charm, like a resort, with an enclosed area off the kitchen, an open porch to sit, and a high lookout porch to observe the pond, the great views of the farmhouse, and the mountains.

After all this work was completed, Michael soon discovered a problem with the shoreline of the adjoining lot—the small peninsula that time created. This changed the flow of the water and the growth of vegetation, causing his land to become swampy. Unfortunately, this has generated a boundary dispute. The shoreline is very small for this property, maybe ten feet at the most, but he has done a beautiful job of working the land to make a pleasant opening to allow swimming and boating from his property.

Mary and Gary Faucher, Lots 67, 68, and 69
164 Long Pond Road

The Fauchers purchased the three lots from Mike Travis, who is a resident of Long Pond and a real estate dealer. Being a visionary, Mike purchased the lots across the road, not knowing exactly what would happen to them or how he would use them in the future. Mary and Gary Faucher lived in the Northwood Narrows for many a years and always wanted a place on Long Pond. This offered them the opportunity to build their dream home. They were able to design their home to fit into the three lots, using the rocks and trees to enhance the property. They love the area and the accessibility; it is almost across from the public landing, which offers them the space to swim and use their kayaks freely.

Trish and Bruce Kelley, Lots 13, 14, and 15
167 Long Pond Road

Jules and Helen Blier of Manchester, New Hampshire, purchased the lots and built in 1972. They decided to build the house in a chalet style, making it their retreat. Three years later, they renovated it into a year-round home. They built bedrooms downstairs to accommodate their two small daughters. They enclosed the deck on the front and opened it up to a large living room. After doing this, they still wanted a deck, so they built one on the side of the home. They also built a two-stall garage off the road, along with a shed. Their home became the pride of Long Pond. In fact, on May 25, 1986, the home was featured in the *New Hampshire Sunday News* Home section.

After the home was featured, Mickey and Preston Marshall purchased it. They were from Massachusetts and wintered in North Carolina. They moved in and loved Long Pond and became very interested and active in the association. They added a three-season room off the large living room, but were denied the availability of putting heat into this area from the town fathers. They added a small open deck on the back facing the road.

The Marshalls resided here about nine years. They began to feel like it was too much to summer in Long Pond and winter in North Carolina, so the parcel of land went up for sale. Bruce and Trish Kelley were longtime residents of Pembroke, New Hampshire, and were looking for a place on a lake. They loved the area and decided to purchase the home from the Marshalls on August 15, 1995. Now they reside half the year in Longboat Key, Florida, and the remaining months at Long Pond. They love to boat on the lake and were the first to have a pontoon boat. Every evening they would set out for a "toot" around the pond with a drink in hand, a wave to all, and a slow ride to say a good evening to all. They have hosted many a potluck supper for the committee at their homestead.

Ronald and Mary Beth Cuomo, Lot 16
169 Long Pond Road

This lot consisted of mainly very large boulders, little vegetation, and hardly any waterfront to speak of and was owned by Ervin H. Stevens of Saco, Maine. It was sold to Ronald and Mary Beth Cuomo from Bellingham, Massachusetts. With a lot of foresight and determination, a beautiful cape-style home was placed on this piece of land. It has a very large deck extending out the back of the home, with stairs going down to the water's edge. A dock was placed in the water to accommodate swimming and boating. They certainly enhanced the small place of land with their flowers, trees, grass, and a rock driveway. It was unfortunate that during the winter of 2008, someone broke into their cottage and walked off with the television and computers. To date they have not turned up. Due to this and a few other issues, a Crime Watch has been set up for the Long Pond area. Ron and Mary Beth have since created two more floors on their home, making it a three-story home; this way they can accommodate their family and friends.

Beach area and boat landing, Lots 17 and 43
223 Long Pond Road

The developer set aside lot 17 for a particular purpose—to be used by the owners of the back lots. This area was originally intended to be a place where Long Pond residents could go to launch their boats. Part of the hill was tarred with black top and then fill was dumped into the pond to create a landing for boats. However, this part of the pond is very, very deep. The more they filled, the more it disappeared because of the drop off. In fact, it is so deep that if you step out six feet from shore, you are instantly in over your head. Therefore, they abandoned the idea.

As time went on, this lot was under discussion; some believed it was unusable land and should be sold. Others, though, held an opposing viewpoint. Many people tried to launch boats there, but because of the incline of the hill, several trucks and cars had to be pulled out. It was then voted to place large boulders in front of the lot so that no automobiles be driven down. It was accomplished. However, when the Cuomos were building, they had to remove the boulders so their house could be placed on the foundation. Today the area is used for swimming as well as rowboats, paddleboats, and so on. The people that form the association in this area have maintained it, and it continues to be a welcoming place to enter the pond, and if desired, a home owner can park his car to unload their kayaks there.

Lot 43
The Association's Public Beach

This section of land has been set aside to allow the back property owners swimming rights to Long Pond. Since this beach is not for public use, only the owners of Long Pond Estates can legally swim there. This beach is maintained by the people and for the people; each year there is a work party held, and several volunteers help with raking, cleaning, and putting out the raft, which was purchased with estate money for the beach. It was strongly suggested that the beach not be used for any boats, large or small. They should be launched at the landing farther down the road. However, many still launch their kayaks there, causing no problems. It is a wonderful place for back-lot owners to gather and swim with their children.

For years the Long Pond Association meetings were held on the beach area and a potluck meal was served. But as the lots were sold and built upon, more and more people attended the meetings and it became increasingly difficult to do this, so it was eliminated from the plan.

However, before this practice was eradicated, there was an incident my husband and I will never forget. It happened the day that we brought our granddaughter, Jennifer, with us. While Paul and I were in the meeting, Jennifer was playing in the water. Being a typical playful child, she decided to climb onto the shoulders of another child. As her friend took a step back, she lost her balance, not realizing the sudden drop-off in that area. Within seconds, Jennifer was underwater. I jumped in along with another person; we quickly surfaced, each holding one of Jennifer's arms. She was safe, and I was grateful. It is amazing how fast things can happen.

David and Miriam Butler, Lot 18
173 Long Pond Road

This lot of land was sold several times; the beginning price was $4,200 when sold, then it went back on the market for $19,000, then it was sold. Then it was put back on the market after the person that purchased it started to clear the land but gave up, and it was back on the Realtor's list, this time for $49,000. It was purchased by Paul and Judith Martyn, of Beverly, Massachusetts, for the price of $45,000.

The Martyns cleared the area but soon discovered the land was built on ledge. Plans for their year-round home were sent before the planning board, but then the problems began. It was sitting on solid rock, so they hired someone to blast the land to achieve enough for an opening for a foundation, which would become a walk-in cellar and a path to the water. They ran into problems with drilling for a well. Ford Well, Inc., from Northwood, New Hampshire, was doing the drilling. They were drilling down near the pond; after a considerable amount of drilling, they finally reached a suitable depth. The strange thing about the land in this whole area is that it is so inconsistent; across the street, when the Ilacquas' well was dug they went down only several hundred feet. They had so much water they had to stop.

It took them three years to build this custom stone-and-cedar lakefront home. They used the stones from the blasting to form a wall and stairs by the lakefront. They also used the blasting stones to create a wall on the right side of the lot, so they could have a built-up septic system to drive upon. From the next property, it appears to be an old-fashioned stone wall.

While they were building, every weekend they would come up and stay in their shed, which was built on the front of the lot to house them. It was cute, and they made it into a neat little camper. As Paul was a master craftsman, much attention was given to detail for this home. Every stone of the two fireplaces, exterior wall, and walkways was handpicked and carefully placed. All the custom wood cabinets, walks, and solid beams were meticulously finished by hand. The unique open floor plan offers an unforgettable space for entertaining or a haven for total relaxation. This home has a towering cathedral ceiling with skylights and one beautiful wall of an eyebrow window facing the south side. After they finished building the home and had moved in, a thief had entered their little shed and removed all the contents; this person was never captured.

Several years later the home was sold to David and Miriam Butler of Boxford, Massachusetts, who are thoroughly enjoying the waterfront home. They have a mix of boats on the waterfront, paddleboats, sailboats, a canoe—nothing that requires a motor; it's all human power. When a large white birch decided to pull out of the ground and fall beside his dock, David was in his paddleboat, cutting the limbs by hand to clean up the mess. Then a man was hired to pull the rest of the trunk out of the water using a come-along and chainsaw.

Sometimes their large sailboat can get them into trouble. For example, one day Dave decided to use the sailboat and was going around very nicely when he decided to go further into the northerly end of the pond. The shape of the pond creates an area where the wind does not blow, and he was stuck. Paul DuPont, my husband, was watching and noticed Dave was not moving. Dave tried paddling with the rudder, but to no avail. So Paul got into his motorboat and went to pull him back. Ever since that episode, Dave watches where he goes and what the wind is doing.

My own family once purchased a small sailboat called a Sunfish. I decided to try the sailboat out. The wind was so strong and took me so quickly I crashed into the neighbor's dock. Guess what? It was sold.

Irene E. and Paul DuPont, Lots 19 and 20
175 Long Pond Road

The original owners, Mr. and Mrs. Harold Stickles, of Florida, purchased the land and the cabin unfinished from the developer. They used the place for two weeks out of the year. They did intend to finish the inside, but never did get to accomplishing it. The water was not even visible from the porch, as many trees and growth of brushes had obstructed the view. They used it as a hideaway. Their daughter had a place on Suncook Pond, where they spent most of their time. In fact, years later their daughter came by to see the cottage and was amazed as to what we did to enhance it.

Working with our children, we opened up the waterfront for swimming and boating. We also painted and finished the inside. The Stickles had left some furniture as well as a new rug and curtains, which were soon hung. We were able to finish furnishing the house with extra furniture they had. The house was transformed into a nice friendly cottage. The lots on either side of them came up for sale, but only one could be purchased. So lot 20, the lot on the right side, was purchased. This lot had many trees to be removed to make space for picnic tables and benches. This was accomplished with time, to complete the look of togetherness. Many changes have occurred on this property, such as an enclosed porch, a new deck on the road side, a modernized kitchen, and walls on the front side with the lawn, stairs to the water, and granite stairs leading to a barbeque pit. Water is drawn from the lake, but drinking water is brought in each week. The cottage became shipshape, for the family to use and enjoy.

Rosalie Ilacqua, Lots 76 and 77
174 Long Pond Road

Helen and Fay Kane, Jr., of Eliot, Maine, purchased this cottage from the developers. They enjoyed the area for swimming as well as hunting. When I talked with Rosalie's son, Jean, he mentioned the newspaper article that hangs on the wall in the camp that reads: "Mr. Fay S. Kane, Jr., of Eliot, Maine, is the envy of all local hunters. He rounded up and shot a ten-point buck weighing 207 lbs., dressed. This happened in the vicinity of Gilford residence in the Narrows."

Rosalie Ilacqua purchased the camp on October 2, 1972. Her interest in the property was due to her sister and bother-in-law (the Gradys), who already owned a camp on the lake. This allowed the lakefront to be available to them for their children to swim and boat. This cottage has the same basic layout as ours but has a total different layout inside, as they have three bedrooms. The cottage has been repainted to a beautiful brown with green trim. This camp is a happy, friendly place and always has family and friends there. Rosalie's son, Jean enjoys the camp and while there, always goes fishing. It is so cute to see him out fishing in his paddleboat. He takes his fishing gear, cooler, and radio and heads to the pond to spend hours out on the water.

One day, upon returning, he and his girlfriend were enjoying a quiet time by the outdoor fire, when Paul said to me, "There is a guy who fell out of his kayak and was trying to hang on to the boat but wasn't having much success. Then he was trying to swim to the large rock in the middle of the pond. It didn't look good." I ran to Jean and asked for help. Paul was getting the oars out of the shed. They ran down to the rowboat, and Jean jumped in and paddled over to him. Jean said, "Hang on to the back of the rowboat." Another kayaker went after the guy's boat, which had floated to the end of the pond. Jean rowed him to the shore, whereby he proceeded to get into the boat so Jean could row him back to his cottage. After leaving him and returning to our shoreline, he hollered to Paul, "Boy, I landed a big one that time!"

Rosaline's property is larger than most in this area because she purchased the lot beside her, lot 76, from Bernard K. Labbe, of Pembroke, New Hampshire. This lot is a pie shape, but it abuts the James right-of-way, so no one can build right up close to the property line.

Jeff Symes and Melissa Pazdon, Lot 78
176 Long Pond Road

This lot was purchased by Tom and Lorraine Home, of Nashua, New Hampshire, from the developer, and then Forrest and Jennifer Brock purchased it. They developed the land by placing a small modular home upon the lot of land, with a septic system in the back. It was then sold to Suzanne Johnston. She is a wonderful artist, who specialized in painting and drawing and produced beautiful jewelry. Being so far from Portsmouth made it hard for her to work in galleries and sell her wares, so she had to sell her home. She enhanced the property by adding a front porch and overhanging roof, adding to the beauty of the home.

The present owners, Jeff Symes and Melissa Pazdon, are also creative people; it seems that the occupants of this home have artistic flairs. They are enhancing the home with a deck and stairs on the side of the residence.

Priscilla Schuyler, Lots 21 and 22
177 Long Pond Road

This A-frame building was one of the original buildings, built as an ideal summer property, and it was known as the pink camp. John and Anna Chute, of Greenfield, New Hampshire, purchased the property and soon added the extra lot. This allowed them to have a U-shaped driveway. It is landscaped in such a way to allow for launching their boat. They had a beautiful wooden inboard motorboat; it was a sure classic. With this they had many family gatherings, boating, water-skiing, and swimming. When winter arrived, they would bring out their snowmobiles and ride the trails in and around the Northwood area. There were many trails around Little Bow, Jenness Pond, and Durgin Pond. These trails would end up at Lake Shore Farms, where many would stay for the night, eating, drinking, and chatting about the trails.

Due to failing health, they sold the camp to Stephen and Priscilla Schuyler, of Kittery Point, Maine. The family changed the color from pink to a chocolate brown, but they weren't happy with that color, so it is now green with a white trim, which enhances it greatly. They have two daughters, who enjoy the swimming and boating, with their friends. Due to an accident during the early winter months, Mr. Schuyler died on the Long Pond Road, where his automobile hit a tree and burnt. Priscilla's parents have worked tirelessly many weekends enhancing the property, replacing the dock, fixing and repairing all that was needed.

Salvatore and Josephine Aiello, Lots 79 and 80
178 Long Pond Road

Salvatore and Josephine Aiello, of Billerica, Massachusetts purchased this land from the developer in 1963. The camp, which was the model style, A-frame construction, was built in 1965, but in 1976 they expanded by adding on two bedrooms and a family living room. They are the original owners, but due to health problems, the cottage is up for sale at the time of this writing.

Sal was instrumental in establishing the Long Pond Association, served several years as president, and helped each and every year on the road cleanup crew. Sal's family has truly enjoyed the pond, swimming and boating, and having many picnics on the front of their property.

Lois Beedenbender and Sara V. Erjavec, Lot 23
181 Long Pond Road

Ethelaine and Robert Henson purchased the lot from Long Pond Estates, Inc., on November 20, 1969, but then Rose and Louis Lamaraca purchased it on December 11, 1969. The land then was purchased by Joseph and Audrey Grady, of Rochester, New Hampshire, on June 16, 1971. They proceeded to build the cottage. They enjoyed the pond for many years as their family grew. Then Joe tried to improve the camp by raising the frame and constructing a cement foundation under it. As the winter approached, he quit for the season. After an extremely bad winter, the runoff from the thaw caused the foundation to crack, and the house began to slide off and go to the side. It was deemed uninhabitable. He became discouraged and later sold the property. Another sad happening occurred to the family while owning there. The oldest son, who flew doing topography maps for the state, died in an airplane crash while on a job.

The property was later purchased by Lois Beedenbender and her daughter, Sara V. Erjavec, of New York. Lois states that when she tried to purchase the property, it was all boarded up. She had telephoned the Gradys to see if they would be interested in selling the property, but they declined. However, a few months later, Mr. Grady contacted her and told her he would be willing to sell for the price of the land, $20,000. Lois then got estimates to rebuild the structure. She settled on Copeland Builders, who said it would be more economic to build a new house rather than try to repair the old. She and her daughter set about designing the home, had plans drawn up, and proceeded to get permits and then went ahead to build. This is a beautiful home with a walk-in basement and a well-designed upstairs to accommodate the family. She had rented from Joanne and Rich Kerns for two years (they resided on the lakeside but a few lots up). She fell in love with the quiet, peaceful setting of the pond and people.

Richard and Jo-Ann Kerns, Lot 26
183 Long Pond Road

Richard and Jo-Ann Kerns, of Baldwin, New York, purchased the land and later had a season home placed upon a foundation. This home has a great deck on the waterfront, allowing for excellent viewing of the lake.

Michael and Rachel Rainey, Lots 24, 25, 81, 82, 83, and 84
186 Long Pond Road

These lots were owned by Marilyn M. Ecker, of Shillington, Pennsylvania, and then Michael and Rachel Rainey, of Northwood, New Hampshire, purchased several parcels of land, built a beautiful log-style home, but they also have two lots on the water allowing them the availability to the pond. They both work for the State Department of Environmental Services, so almost every year, the pond water gets tested. The test has always proved the pond water is acceptable and great for swimming.

Meredith and Frederick L. Langevin Jr., Lot 27
189 Long Pond Road

Owners Frederick and Meredith Langevin, of Concord, New Hampshire, purchased this lot from Frederick and Maureen Fenton; she was a well-known weaver in New Hampshire. The Fentons purchased the cottage from Bernadette Brooks on June 30, 1980. The Brooks son was the contractor, who built the cottage for them after purchasing the land from Gerald H. and Ruby M. Giles on March 26, 1962.

On the day of the signing the cottage a comedy of errors occurred. As they were about to sign the papers of transfer, they saw that the wives' names were reversed. So the agent had to take them back and make the changes. Meredith said to her husband, Fred, "If I had known he was throwing his wife in on the deal, we could have made him a better offer."

The Langevins tell about their granddaughter Jessie Dulude, who spent her summers with them at Long Pond. She was introduced to theater camp at the Masonic Hall, in Northwood Narrows, which was run by Rebecca Rule's daughter, Adie. She attended the camp for four summers and appeared in four of their original musicals. Many of the friends at Long Pond attended the performances, which were a hit. The camp was called Dinosaur in a Dish. During the summers, she made many close friends.

Ellen and Kurt Schreiber, Lots 28 and 29
191 Long Pond Road

James and Denise Viar purchased this A-frame house and lived there for many years; they never changed the design and layout. Then Mark Forman and Kathleen Secrest purchased the house and proceeded to do many, many changes in its appearance and shape. During this period of time, the house became known as "the house of seven gables." It went up for sale, and Ellen and Kurt Schreiber purchased the property and made more changes. It has a very interesting shape and design. Many people today still refer to this house as the seven-gable home. This land mass also has a very different shape. The land juts out into a curved shape with a sandy beach area almost like a peninsula, allowing for a very convenient place to leave their kayaks on or swim.

Paul and Victoria Lesnyk, Lots 30, 31, 85, 86, and 87
190 Long Pond Road

Paul and Victoria Lesnyk were among the original owners of a Long Pond estate. They purchased two lots on the water, with a camp built on the land. Years later they purchased a year-round home, which was built across the road. This is a beautiful two-story cape. There was a consistent argument with the association because they owned two homes, one on the water and one on the road, but they continued to pay one fee, until a lien was placed on their property by the president of the association.

Due to a conflict, a lien had also been placed upon our property because of seventy-five dollars. It was suggested that stickers be given to the Long Pond residents because outsiders were parking on the road and using the beach areas. Russell Eldridge gave me the authorization to purchase the stickers. I had them printed and disturbed them to the owners and turned the bill into the association. They did not refund the seventy-five dollars, so I removed it from my dues. The president of the association then placed a lien on the property for this money.

Therefore our families went before a lawyer to resolve this matter of removing the liens. As no formal letter or any form of notice was sent to either family, we hired a lawyer to represent us. In the end, the association agreed to remove the liens, the matter closed, with no payment due. The association learned from this event; they had to pay out for a lawyer and pull back on placing liens on properties without first notifying the parties. This could have been avoided if certain people had come together, listened to the problem, and solved it.

At the time of this writing, the Lesnyks are clearing the pond side land and rebuilding the cottage on the water's edge. This will certainly be a beautiful homestead with a beautiful view on the pond.

Joshua and Natalia Beaullieu, Lot 32
194 Long Pond Road

This home was built by Robert and Helen Hotchkiss, of Northwood, New Hampshire. When they purchased the land, Robert and Helen owned a large farm in Northwood, so they proceeded to cut and mill the trees into board feet. Using the wood from his farmland, he built his two bedroom home on Long Pond. They resided only half a year in Northwood and spent the rest in Florida after their farm was sold. Bob always had a small garden up front on the road. He took great pride in producing his vegetables. The home was sold when Robert passed away and Helen was placed in assisted living. Darren and Roxanne Finch purchased the home. Then it was later sold to Christine Legault and Russell Trudel, who added a three-season porch and a deck. It was sold again to Joshua and Natalia Beaullieu. Many changes have taken place within the framework of this building.

Barbara Bock and Jan Dipaolo, Lots 33 and 34
201 Long Pond Road

These lots were once owned by Russell and Jo Eldridge, of Northwood, New Hampshire, but are now owned by Barbara Bock and Jan Dipaolo, who love the area and the community.

Mr. Russell was one of the early founders of the Long Pond Association; in fact, he was the treasurer for many, many years, and he was one of the people who worked to help keep the road in good condition. He had a tractor, which he would use to even out rough spots in the road. Upon selling the cottage, he and his wife Jo purchased a homestead on Route 4, still in the town of Northwood.

Scott and Kathryn Behner, Lot 35
203 Long Pond Road

This land was owned by Elizabeth F. Gustafson and John Feder, of Dayton, Ohio, when it was sold to them. This couple built a two-story home facing the pond. They are avid water-skiers and ski in the large area of the pond, providing a wonderful show for the entire shoreline to view. They have a permit from the state to keep the buoys in the water. The buoys are at the bottom of the lake and rise to the top when run by a compressor that is situated on a family friend's property; when skiers are finished, they go down.

John F. Lyskawa, Lot 36
205 Long Pond Road

This property was purchased by Shirley Tweedell, of Concord, New Hampshire, who used it as a summer camp until she decided to add on a second story and make it a year-round home. This took place over a period of time and finally, they sold their home in Concord and moved in permanently. She raised her three children and her husband's two children there. Long Pond was a wonderful place for them to enjoy many summer and winter sports. After many years, when the children had moved on, it was sold to Jill Linzee, who lived there for a short time and then sold it to John F. Lyskawa. He completely removed all the interior walls and several of the outside walls. Bill Tweedell, the contractor, had not built the second story well enough; it needed to be reinforced, as the second story was listing. This home has a beautiful frontage on the water and a long driveway coming off the road, giving much privacy.

Richard and Monette Lamontagne, Lot 37
207 Long Pond Road

Richard and Monette Lamontagne purchased the land from Charles Jafforian in 1986 and proceeded to build their cute little home.

Orphy and Mindy Cheung, Lot 38
211 Long Pond Road

This home was owned by Palmer and Verna McWilliams but has been sold to Orphy and Melinda Cheung, from Massachusetts. Using the A-frame as the base, they are building up and out making a large addition for their family. The land abuts their neighbors with a wonderful bridge over a small stream.

Stephen Soucy and Ronda Sylvester, Lot 39
213 Long Pond Road

This family's homestead is totally different from the norm, as they have refinished what was a basement into a beautiful home. They also own the lot across from them, which has been made into a two-stall garage with rooms above. Beautiful landscaping has been added to enhance the property.

Dick and Jackie LeCompte, Lots 41 and 42
221 Long Pond Road

This home abuts the public beach area; the driveways are separate, but side by each. It was owned by the Pineros for several years, and it is now owned by Dick and Jackie LeCompte, of 13 Mont Vernon Dr., Londonderry, New Hampshire. They have worked hard to enhance their property on the shore.

William R. Faulkner, Lot 44 and 45
225 Long Pond Road

The original owners were Ira and Corinne Levy; it was then purchased by Herbert and Marie Dodge, on November 11, 1977, then William R. Faulkner, of Concord, New Hampshire, purchased the cottage on September 5, 1979. Mr. Faulkner is the treasurer of the Long Pond

Property Owners and does a splendid job. This home is not winterized, so Bill uses it only for the warm summer months. It is a neat little cottage placed in such a way that the trees surround it; in fact, some trees offer a type of stairway to the back porch. Although it abuts the public beach area, there are many trees that offer privacy from beachgoers. He always has a well-kept flower garden in front of his property on the side of the driveway, which has a charming appeal.

Carl and Eileen Golden, Lots 46 and 47
229 Long Pond Road

This property is owned by Carl and Eileen Golden, from New York State. They have been the original owners since the development started. They now live in Northwood full-time. Carl served as one of officers of the association for many years, as well as overseeing the cleanup crew, which normally works one week after the annual meeting in July. Carl was one of the founding fathers of the association and very instrumental in establishing the by-laws.

Rick and Theresa Barisano, Lots 104 and 105
234 Long Pond Road

This cottage was once owned by the Russells. The family loved the area for many reasons—snowmobiling in the winter and water sports in the summer. The Russells did have a problem with the association rules; it occurred when they put large posts in the roadway in front of their property as decoration. This presented a large problem when winter came, and the plows could not get by. That was the era where they only went to the V in the road, as no year-round cottages were up above. The Russells were required to move the posts back onto their property. This property was later sold to Rick and Theresa Barisano, who upgraded it with a lot of improvements and a paint job.

Bruce Cronhard, Lots 48, 49, 50, 51, 51, 52, and 110
12 Lookout Point

This property has a different street name, as it is a V off the main road and had to be posted differently for fire and emergency reasons. This land was originally purchased by Edward Shinn and his wife, a wonderful artist and designer. They built a fortress-style home, but later as they decided to live there year round, many additions were made to the home. It was said that after he first built, kids broke in and destroyed the inside, so he had to rebuild the interior. With all the land he owned, he built a garage the size of another home. Then a shed was added to accommodate lawn furniture and equipment. The area for swimming wasn't great; being at the lower end of the pond, it allowed for the growth of pond lilies. Ed added large stones on the front, creating a type of wall, which enhanced the beauty of the home. When Ed's wife took very ill, they had to sell and move back to Marblehead, Massachusetts, where they were originally from. Ed was also one of the founding fathers of the association and accomplished so much, setting rules and regulations in place. He loved to debate on a variety of subjects when they were presented at the meeting, just to get people thinking and speculating about them. This home was purchased by Bruce Cronhard and Barry Headings. Sadly, Barry had a massive heart attack and passed on.

Ron and Lydia Lamontagne, Lots 49A and 50A
239 Long Pond Road

This cottage is situated on the V of the two roads, Lookout Point and Long Pond Road. Before the Lamontagnes purchased the place, it was owned by Al Dryer, who was also one of the founding fathers of the association. Al was one who was always arguing at the meetings regarding money, trying to get the members to establish stocks and bonds. He and Ed Shinn would always go head-to-head. When the cottage went up for sale, Ron and Lydia purchased it. They have done a great deal of work enhancing this property; they closed in the porch, and added new stairs and new siding. Many trees have been cut due to their size and danger of falling on the home. This was once considered the end of the road, but progress and development moved the end of the road up the hill.

Mark Vail, Lots 106, 107, and 108
240 Long Pond Road

This cottage has quite a history to it. When it was built, it was built close to the line. The dispute began with the Russells stating it was to close, but nothing was done about it. The septic system was put in on the property line. So Russells filled the system with cement, rendering it useless. The people had to move out. John Gaudet, Jr., purchased the home and was living there, but because it had a mold problem, it was labeled unlivable. So John moved out and is renting on Long Pond. John has volunteered to assist the road agent in maintaining the road for the Long Pond Association. Mark Vail is the present owner of this cottage.

Nate and Kristie Torbick
253 Long Pond Road

As the story goes, this lot of land was donated to the public television auction. Stephanie Cotrell and Steve Giordani bid on it and received it at auction. They cleared the land and built a very unique home, but as they had two children, it proved to be too small. They sold it many years later to Nate and Kristie Torbick. This lot goes all the way to the water, but the shoreline is filled with pond lilies, making it difficult to swim or boat.

Ernie Croto, Lots 54 and 55
261 Long Pond Road

This little cottage was built by a Northwood town clerk, who purchased the land from the developer and built a small camp about the size of a large shed; it was used for several years. Thomas O'Donnell, of Connecticut, then purchased it and built a large year-round home facing the water. In 1998, Deborah and Robert Diamond purchased the cottage and lived there for many years. They sold it to Mr. Croto, who now resides at this beautiful home. Due to the layout of the land, it has a rather steep driveway down to the pond.

Paul and Amy Lindsay, Lots 56, 57, and 58
265 Long Pond Road

The original owners were Dick and Barbara McSherry, of Florida; they built the home facing the lake, with a long sweeping driveway going down and around the land. They built a garage at the top of the road, so they could access it easily. The land was a difficult piece of property because of the steep slope of the hill. It was later sold to Richard Lammers and Katherine Rannie from Durham, New Hampshire, then sold to Paul and Amy Lindsay. They have continued to improve the landscape with more additions and clever ways to the water. Amy has maintained the blueberry trees growing near the shoreline, and they have produced quite a harvest of fruit.

Chy and Sandi Souryanvong, Lots 113 and 114
260 Long Pond Road

This homestead had a strange beginning. A man applied to the town to build a house on these two lots, and it was approved. Then the association granted him permission to live in the camper while building, as it is written in the quitclaim deed that you cannot place a camper on the land for year-round living. Everyone was worried, as several years went by before a house appeared. Finally it was finished, the camper disappeared, and it was sold to Chy.

Mary Beale and Susanne Fortier, Lots 100,101,102, and 103
228 Long Pond Road

Mary Beale and Susanne Fortier purchased this little red A-frame cottage that sat right on the road, in front of the public beach area; they used it as a summer retreat. It was the original model for the developer to entice buyers. As time went by they decided to add a room on to the back of the building to create more space, but because it was right on the road, dirt and dust were continually flying in as autos drove by. Finally they decided to rebuild; they moved up the land and built a beautiful chalet home with much space and glamour. It is beautifully landscaped and a creative piece of architecture. They were fortunate to acquire additional lots, increasing the size of property and adding charm and beauty to the new homestead.

Roger and Marianne Cussins
269 Long Pond Road

This is one lot that did not belong to the Long Pond developer. I was given to understand the land belonged to Maurice James, and he sold it separately to an individual. A home was built with the understanding that a loop would be established to allow vehicles to turn around at the end of the road. This was never completed, the home went into disrepair, and the owners left. Roger Cussins then purchased the parcel of land and the home. He has completely renovated the home and created a beautifully landscaped property with stone walls and plants. A garage was built off the road for easy access. He did finish the end of the road. Roger has been very active in keeping the whole length of the road in good repair.

CHAPTER 9

FAMILY EVENTS

Our family of five children enjoyed the shore, boating, water-skiing, fishing, and swimming. Two weddings occurred on the property. Our daughter Cynthia planned her marriage to Mark Otterson to be held on the dock by the water, but due to rain, we decided to call the Lake Shore Farms, on Jenness Pond. They had a time slot of a few hours in their conference center that we could use for the marriage ceremony. It worked out perfectly, and the reception was still held at the cottage.

Years later, our son William wanted to get married at the camp on the dock; this marriage was also in October. He was very fortunate, as the weather was holding; in fact, the day of the wedding was a beautiful sunny and warm day. The area was decorated with corn husks and pumpkins. Paul and Judy Martyn, the next-door neighbor, allowed Dawn, the bride, to dress at their place. The bride, the bridesmaid, Dawn's sister, and the flower girl, Willow, walked down the brick path to the dock. A family friend, Priscilla Masse, sang for the ceremony. The reception was held at the cottage, and all enjoyed the festivities.

As we love the outdoors and fishing, we quickly discovered the beauty of owning a home on Long Pond. Within minutes, they were ready to go to the boat, cast a line to catch a bass, perch, pickerel, and other kinds of fish. This tranquil setting was the perfect place to unwind and enjoy the wonders of nature. The children really loved to fish; when they weren't swimming, they were throwing in a line, testing their luck at catching the biggest one. Dad's plug was the favorite; it was a popper that looked like a frog.

Jennifer Tasker, with her many

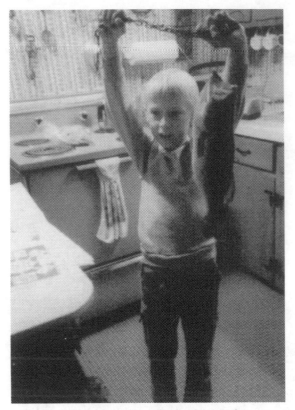

Michael Blichmann, his big catch

One of the largest bass ever caught was hooked by Paul's oldest daughter, Roxanne. That was a day we will never forget. We were at the Long Pond Association's annual meeting, held at the public beach area; it was July 4, 1978. All of a sudden, Roxanne came running to the beach, yelling, and holding up the fish with the hook and line still secured. The line, still trailing yards behind, was a sight to behold. The crazy part was the reel had broken, so to hang onto the fish and bring it in, she had to run up the hill, pulling the line with the large bass on the other end. She landed it on the grassy part of the land. Excited by her unexpected feat, she was bubbling up with enthusiasm. She wanted a keepsake; that's when we decided to trace it on to newspaper. Later it was cut out of a pine board, carved with her name, the date, and the size of the fish—19½ inches, 4 pounds. The board went up, and it was the start of our porch gallery.

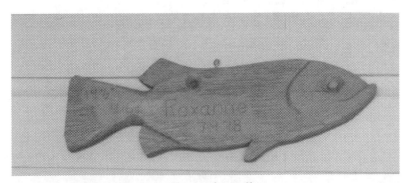

First on the wall

More proud fishermen followed. These photographs show other members of the family with their catches. The household rule is, "You catch it; we eat it or throw it back."

Paul DuPont, Senior

Ulric DuPont, father

Ice fishing is another sport our family has always enjoyed. It was the challenge of chopping a hole in the ice and placing the tip-ups in, with high hopes of catching something. It was usually a pickerel, since they were the favorite caught during the winter months. This was made into wonderful fish chowder. Here is Roxanne enjoying the weather, waiting for a tip-up to occur.

The sun was so warm.

FISH CHOWDER

1 small onion, sliced
4 potatoes peeled and cubed
4 cups of water
1 cup of milk
1 can of evaporated milk
4 tablespoon of butter
3 tsp of salt pork, fried to a brown crisp
3 slices of American cheese, or more to thicken the stock
1 lb of fish or a good-sized one, chunked
Salt and pepper to taste

Added water to potatoes and onions; boil till soft. Add evaporated milk, whole milk, and butter. Prepare salt pork by frying it till brown and crispy. Add to milk and potatoes and stir. Drop each slice of cheese in separately and stir; if you want it thicker, add more cheese. Simmer slowly. Now add the chunked fish carefully; stir very slowly for fifteen minutes. Add salt and pepper to taste.

Do not boil. Stir slowly until the fish is cooked. Enjoy!

The fish now caught in Long Pond and surrounding ponds have been found to have high levels of mercury, according to an article published in the *New Hampshire Sunday News,* on February 19, 2012, by Eric Oriff, current Fish and Game commissioner. He stated within this article that all the water bodies that were downwind of the Bow power plant have unacceptable levels of mercury. Fish caught in any of these waters are dangerous to human health if eaten.

Another nice treat was going hornpout fishing. This was a family outing; we were armed with worms, string hooks made by Paul, which consisted of a small stick with a heavy string wrapped around it and a large hook on the end with a heavy sinker, a lantern, and mosquito repellent. Out in the boat, we would go to one of the coves, as they had the muddy bottoms. We would set up in the early evening, throw the lines in, and wait for a bite. We would catch the biggest hornpouts to truly enjoy a meal the next morning.

We would sometimes catch an eel. They create a mess, especially if pulled into the boat, which occasionally would happen. Paul would say, "If you think it is an eel, don't pull it in the boat; hold it to the side while we disarm it." An eel is like a snake, twisting and curling around the line. If they are brought in to the boat, the eel will swirl around, moving quickly, causing turmoil. Not to mention . . . they are slimy, slippery, and hard to handle. But if a situation developed, Paul would disarm them and place them into the bucket to go home to our neighbor. She is of German descent and knows how to cook the eels. She and her husband always enjoyed eating them.

Fishing was always a highlight of our camping experience, as was hunting. We always looked forward to October 1, the first day of bird hunting. As a family, we would head out to the camp and bring the canoe or the rowboat and decoys. Then we'd set up, performing our traditional "duck walk," a term coined by Mr. Shinn, who would anxiously watch for us to set up the decoys. These would naturally attract the ducks to the water. Then the hunt would begin!

The three ponds in our Northwood area gave us a great advantage for duck hunting. Our dog was trained to retrieve any ducks that were shot down. Our yellow Lab, Shotgun, was trained to get in and out of the canoe or boat without tipping it. She was a great dog, and with unending patience, she would sit and wait until it was time for her to move into action.

One morning while setting up to hunt, Paul was on one side and I was on the other. He called and said, "Send the dog." She left but did not go to him; instead, she came back to me, carrying a duck. Neither of us had fired a shot, but she had retrieved a beautiful mallard. We laughed about it, as she'd had her own hunting experience. We would always find her waiting in the canoe to go for another hunting journey.

Waiting to go

Hunting wasn't limited to only ducks. We also hunted pheasant and woodcock when in season, especially around the area of Northwood. Deer hunting was also a fall sport. Many of the family members would gather at the camp, starting out very early in the morning, heading out to find the deer; they were not always successful, but a good time was had by all. These two photographs show proud hunters, Lionel April, Paul's cousin from Manchester, who now resides in Florida, and our son Robert, with his pheasant.

Lionel April with his deer   *Robert DuPont with his pheasant*

Our youngest son, Billy, and his friends would also try their hand at fishing. These photographs show their catch and their friendship.

Friendship: Shawn McKay and Billy DuPont.

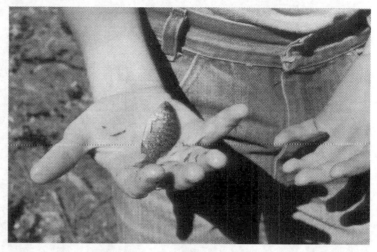

Look at my catch!

Surprise

I love to surprise my husband with different things. One day on my way to the cottage, I discovered a large snapping turtle laying her eggs in the sand by the outlet to Durgins Pond. This seemed like the perfect opportunity to rescue the turtle and surprise Paul.

I backed my Buick Skylark to where she was. opened my trunk, gathered her up by the shell, and placed her into my trunk. Using a container I had in my car, I carefully collected some eggs and sand, which I later brought to the science department at Nashua High, where I was employed. When I first arrived at the cottage, I yelled for Paul, telling him, "I have a surprise for you in the trunk of my car." He opened the trunk cover and exclaimed, "What?" Then I looked, and to my surprise, nothing was there. She had crawled up into the wheel well of the car. It took several hours to get her out. We finally did. The next day we enjoyed a hearty bowl of turtle soup, and her shell was placed in our trophy room back home. The best part was that the Nashua High students enjoyed delivering ten baby turtles, which grew and were returned to the Mill Pond near the school.

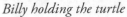

Billy holding the turtle   *Paul holding another turtle that was captured*

Ladder

As a family, including the dog, we enjoyed taking a walk around Little Bow, looking for deer tracks and getting our exercise. We often did this in the late afternoon. Now we have walked these pathways many, many times. One time we came across a twenty-foot wooden ladder lying in the path. Where did this come from? Whom did it belong to? Why was it on the path? Why was it in the woods? It came back to the cottage with us. We posted it, tried to find the owner. We still have the ladder.

Winning Photo

Father's Day came, and all the family gathered at the cottage to celebrate the day with a barbeque and cake. Paul had always kidded about the hard, cold bathroom seat. So as a gift, the children purchased a foam padded seat to replace the wood one as a joke. It was bright yellow. After Paul opened the gift, Jennifer, our granddaughter, was there, and Paul placed it in front of her as frame. She was not too happy about this and proceeded to pout. I snapped the photograph. When I read in the *Manchester Union Leader* that Kodak was sponsoring a photo contest, I decided to enter that picture.

I was surprised and elated to win first prize, which came with money and a beautiful pewter plate celebrating Kodak's bicentennial. This photo went on to Kodak in Rochester, New York, and won a national award.

Father's Day.

Swimming

In the early morning or late evening, if one watches very carefully, you might see a deer or two swimming across the body of water. This happens quite often in the large area of the pond. They don't like to walk on the land area. They seem to come across from the Little Durgin area along the canal. We were out fishing when we saw one swimming; in fact, we thought at first it might be a dog, but it was a young doe. We proceeded to be very careful approaching it, so as to not scare it, but it swam away and landed upon the opposite shore.

Deer was swimming

Shotgun, a Wonderful Dog

This yellow lab was a most remarkable animal. She would hunt with us, capturing and delivering with pride and love whatever fowl it was. She would retreat into her wine-barrel doghouse and watch; she would greet people in the most unusual way. As you can see by the photograph, the jumping up and down would begin, but she would never jump on you.

Welcome, welcome

CHAPTER 10

ICE HAS ITS OWN STORY

When I think of all the fun we have had with snow and ice as a winter sport, ice fishing, snowshoeing, cross-country skiing, and using snow machines, we tend to forget how winter was used in the 1800s. Ice was used for cooling, producing, and preserving foods. This procedure goes back to George Washington and Thomas Jefferson, who had their own personal icehouses. *Take Care at the Barn* states that on several occasions in 1902, Orrin and Charles Small went to cut ice on Durgin's Pond. When finished, they would place their ice cutting in their own icehouse. They used the sawdust from the woodcutting mill to insulate the ice; this would keep it from melting. Harvesting ice became a big business in New England during the nineteenth century. And just as ice was cut on Durgin's Pond, so was ice cut on Long Pond.

In talking with a resident of Long Pond, she related to me a story about ice cutting that occurred one spring in the early 1900s. As the weather was warming, the ice was thinning, and the workers tried to get one more load of ice from the pond before the day ended. It was one load too many. As they were on their way to the shore on the Route 107 side, a thinning spot caused the teams of horses, including the driver and load of ice, to sink to the bottom of the pond. Since the pond is very deep in the middle, estimated at roughly fifty-two feet or so, nothing could be done to save the man, horses, or wagon. It is believed that this site became their final resting place.

Harvesting ice was quite a procedure. I heard about an Ice-Cutting Celebration at Sutton, New Hampshire, being held by the Musterfield farm owners on a Sunday in January. They were also sponsoring a pancake breakfast to raise money for the town's youth group. The collage of photographs display the procedure, from cutting the ice, floating the cube, lifting it, and finally packing it in sawdust at the icehouse. This event was very educational and enjoyable. They used various tools such as pole hook, ice thongs, colander shovel, tree rods, and most important was the boom to remove the ice sections from the water, placing them in the wagon to be hauled to the prepared icehouse.

college of ice farming

A collage of photographs regarding ice cutting

CHAPTER 11

EVENTS IN THE AREA

Johnson's Dairy Farm

Mr. Johnson was a dairy farmer in Northwood, New Hampshire, for years, and I had always enjoyed driving by his farm and land, seeing the animals in the pasture grazing. I was working on a documentary project for the book, *New Hampshire Photographs: The Portrait and the Environment,* spearheaded by Gary Samson. I asked Mr. Johnson if I could photograph him with his cows. He was very receptive of the project and informed me to set my tripod up in a certain area of the field, so as he walked out of the barn with the cows, I could document it. He informed me the animals would not bother me or even notice. Well, there I was aiming my camera and starting to shoot when they all decided to come and see me. Suddenly surrounded by huge animals, I stood still; I was petrified. He started to holler. Then, using a stick, he guided them along to follow the leader. All was fine. Anyone could tell he loved those animals. He was proud of his work, producing milk and raising calves.

Birthing Event (1980)

I never expected to witness the birth of a calf on my way to the Northwood Market, but one afternoon, I was on my way to pick up a few items for our evening meal, and as I traveled down the road, I noticed Mr. Johnson and his helper out in the field, trying to assist a cow that was giving birth. I stopped, armed with a camera and set up to photograph the event. Three young children from New York were there. Their eyes were wide open with anticipation. This was a first for them. However, something was wrong. The calf was not in the birth canal properly. Mr. Johnson had to go in with his hands, trying to turn the baby and put it in the correct position. Then he placed chains on the hoofs so he could pull the calf out. They worked for several hours. After the birth, the mother lay down and then proceeded to clean the little one. The three children were taken by the whole experience. They were petting and talking to the mother, consoling her. It was a wonderful, photographic experience.

Mr. Johnson pulling the calf out.

Consoling the mother.

Since the writing of this book, the farm has stopped production, but the saddest event was in 2009, when his home and first barn burned down, leaving a silo and back barn.

The Annual Work Day

This is a yearly event. The weekend after the annual meeting, volunteers meet and work together to care for the road by clearing away growth on the edges, trimming the trees that could create a problem for the winter months. Men and women show up armed with cutters, chainsaws, grass whips, and so forth. It's always a good group of neighbors who work together to clear the areas of brushes, fallen trees, and whatever else needs to be done. This keeps the sides of the road clear for winter plowing. The members of the association show up at the mailbox ready to work. It always ends with a tired crew but a happy bunch, and the road is ready for another winter.

Expeditions

One of Long Pond's residents, Vito "Chic" Mensale, was one of the early settlers. He always welcomed everyone to the community. He was always seen riding his bicycle up and down the Long Pond road. He was an authority on mushrooms and blueberries. He would take friends and family members out with him, teaching them what was edible and what was not. He spent a great deal of time teaching his grandsons about the beavers and their dam building, something they continue to benefit from today. His grandson, Gary Bates, is one of the keepers of the canal.

CHAPTER 12

DISAPPOINTING NEWS

Although fishing was one of our favorite sports, a new problem has occurred over the last few years regarding the fish in the area lakes and ponds. According to the article by Eric Orff, all the water bodies that were downwind of the Bow power plant have unacceptable levels of mercury. All these waters are dangerous to human health if the fish that are caught are eaten. So the lesson to be learned is catch and release; don't eat. This sign is posted on the tree at Durgin Pond.

Is it safe to eat the fish?

Despite the problem with the fish, Long Pond is by far one of the most beautiful bodies of water around. It contains two small islands. The larger island is often occupied by people camping on it overnight, building a small fire, and enjoying the quietness of the night. This island has a flat surface with several open areas, but most of the outer edge is surrounded by granite rocks. The other island is quite small, surrounded by lilies and grasses, making it almost impossible to land on it. The pond water, being a light tea color, is still very clear. It is spring fed. The depth goes from two feet to fifty five feet in some areas; in most areas it has a rocky bottom, but one end and a few corners are quite swampy, filled with pond lilies and grasses. It is a body of water enjoyed in so many different ways.

BIBLIOGRAPHY

Bailey, Joann Weeks. *A Guide to the History and Old Dwelling Places of Northwood, New Hampshire.* Portsmouth, New Hampshire: Peter E. Randall, 1992.

Northwood, New Hampshire, Route 4, Tax Collectors, Town Tax Office, Copy of Long Pond Development

ABOUT THE AUTHOR

Irene E. DuPont, a photography and art teacher, taught for thirty-five years at Nashua High School, in Nashua, New Hampshire. Since her retirement, Irene has continued her photography and other artistic endeavors. She is also the author of *Spanning Time: New Hampshire Covered Bridges.* Irene has been married to Paul for forty years, and they have five children. Her home is in Manchester, New Hampshire.